FIRE

AND

BREAD

Also by Ruth Burgess:

A Book of Blessings
At Ground Level (out of print)
Candles & Conifers
Eggs and Ashes (with Chris Polhill)
Friends and Enemies
Hay & Stardust
Hear My Cry
Praying for the Dawn (with Kathy Galloway)

FIRE
AND
BREAD

Resources for Easter Day to Trinity Sunday

Ruth Burgess

WILD GOOSE PUBLICATIONS

Contents of book © the individual contributors
Compilation © 2006 Ruth Burgess

First published 2006, reprinted 2010
Wild Goose Publications, 4th Floor, Savoy House, 140 Sauchiehall St, Glasgow G2 3DH, UK.
Wild Goose Publications is the publishing division of the Iona Community.
Scottish Charity No. SC003794. Limited Company Reg. No. SC096243.
www.ionabooks.com
ISBN 978-1-905010-30-1
Cover painting and internal illustration © Scott Riley

The publishers gratefully acknowledge the support of the Drummond Trust,
3 Pitt Terrace, Stirling FK8 2EY in producing this book.

Overseas distribution:
Australia: Willow Connection Pty Ltd, Unit 4A, 3-9 Kenneth Road, Manly Vale, NSW 2093
New Zealand: Pleroma, Higginson Street, Otane 4170, Central Hawkes Bay
Canada: Novalis/Bayard Publishing & Distribution, 10 Lower Spadina Ave., Suite 400,
Toronto, Ontario M5V 2Z2

Printed by Bell & Bain, Thornliebank, Glasgow

GENERAL CONTENTS

Introduction   17

Easter Day   19

Resurrection, laughter and new life   47

Resurrection appearances   79

Opening and closing responses for Eastertide   119

Ascension Day   137

Pentecost   147

Holy Spirit   167

Saints' days   177

Trinity   199

Environmental days   213

Joining Church   221

Making and keeping promises   231

Being Church   239

I am   253

Eucharist, feasting and celebration   265

Community   285

Creation and new life   309

The Bible in about an hour   321

Songs and prayers for the journey   337

Sources and acknowledgements   345

Contributors   349

Index of authors   355

6

CONTENTS IN DETAIL

Easter Day   19

(((◎)))   Opening and closing responses for Easter Day   20
        Give thanks that God is good
        Glory to God
♫   Easter glory fills the heaven   20
✍   An Easter Communion   21
✟   On those times (An Easter confession)   23
𝄞   A new day   24
♫   Lord of Life and Resurrection   25
✍   Very early in the morning   26
♫   Lord, we have seen you walking   31
📖   Among the children (Easter Sunday sermon, Iona Abbey, 2006)   32
   ✢   *The Syrophoenician woman's story   32*
   ✢   *Blind Bartimaeus's story   33*
   ✢   *The Samaritan woman's story   35*
   ✢   *The story of the boy with the loaves and fishes   36*
   ✢   *Mary's story   37*
   ✟   *Prayer (Looking in the wrong places)   38*
✟   Risen, glorious Christ   40
✟   We thought we had heard it all (Lord, have mercy on us)   41
(((◎)))   Risen Christa   43
♫   For it is by your love   44

Resurrection, laughter and new life   47

♫   For now I am making you hear new things   48
✍   Liturgy for Holy Humour Sunday   49
(((◎)))   Newness of life   52
✢   Story snapshots   52
    Heard the news? (Coo, what a pong!)   52
    Mary   54
    Thomas   54
    The graveyard superintendent   55
    Jesus   55
    Martha   56
    The mourners   57

Lazarus 58
The Lazarus story – the official view 58
🖹 Tillie 60
✟ This day 61
✟ God of the purple robe 61
🎜 Shatter the box 62
🎭 Question time 63
✟ Easter offering 65
🎜 The invitation of Easter 66
🎜 Hide and seek 67
🎜 Towards freedom 67
✟ Prayers of the heart 68
🎵 Easter story 69
🖹 Miracle in O'Meara Street 70
🎵 Here in the heart of God 72
🎜 Show and tell 73
🎜 Easter '78 74
🎜 Reflections at Easter 74
🎜 Miss Prince 76
🎜 The moribund Church 76
🎜 It's not even news 77
🎜 The spring cycle 78
✟ A blessing 78

Resurrection appearances 79
🎜 Resurrection 80
❖ What a morning! 81
🎜 Easter haikus 82
❖ Resurrection encounters: 83
Mary Magdalene 83
The upper room 84
Driftwood 84
Thomas 85
Simon Peter 85
✟ Encounter 86
🎭 Peter and Mary 87
🎵 Emmaus way 90
🎭 Two friends 90

Key to symbols
✟ Prayer
🎜 Reading
❖ Biblical reflection
🎵 Liturgy
(((•))) Responses
🎵 Song
🖹 Story
📖 Sermon
🎭 Drama
🚲 Practical
❤ Meditation

🕉   An Emmaus Road liturgy of commitment from Iona Abbey   92

✝   Prayers on the Emmaus Road   94

✝   Emmaus Road   96

♫   Emmaus now   97

🕮   I know that my Redeemer liveth   103

⁘   Thomas's story   105

📖   Scars reveal resurrection   106

⁘   Acts of the apostles   108

     Peter: Transformation   108

     Thomas: My twin   109

     Stephen: Holy ground   109

     On the road   110

     Resident aliens   110

     Times of refreshing   110

♫   The picnic   111

⁘   At the lakeside   112

🕮   Early this morning   114

✝   Eastertide prayers of intercession   115

	Key to symbols
✝	Prayer
🕮	Reading
⁘	Biblical reflection
🕉	Liturgy
((◯))	Responses
♫	Song
🎭	Story
📖	Sermon
🎭	Drama
🚲	Practical
♥	Meditation

Opening and closing responses for Eastertide   119

((◯))   In the breaking of bread and in prayers   120

((◯))   A great mercy and a sure hope   120

((◯))   You take us seriously   120

((◯))   Open our eyes to you amongst us   121

((◯))   The light is shining   121

((◯))   Coming and going   121

((◯))   Sharing stories, sharing food   122

((◯))   We are travelling the way of justice   122

((◯))   Come and hear   122

((◯))   We are not alone: God's love is with us   123

((◯))   Old and young   123

((◯))   Named as Christians   123

((◯))   What do Christians do?   124

((◯))   In us, among us   124

((◯))   What can bring us happiness?   125

((◯))   Love of God   125

((◯))   We are witnesses   125

((◯))   Children of God   126

((O))   Holy and just   126

((O))   In the midst of creation   127

((O))   Heard and valued   127

((O))   God is a God of grace and salvation   128

((O))   Into our streets and homes we go   128

((O))   In my living and in my loving   129

((O))   Growing in us   129

((O))   Sometimes believing, sometimes doubting   130

((O))   As God sent Jesus   130

((O))   In the night and in the morning   130

((O))   Take our hands in your hands   131

((O))   Whoever we are   131

((O))   When our way is joyful   131

((O))   God is loving and full of kindness   132

((O))   Day by day   132

((O))   We come to a holy God   133

((O))   Love God   133

((O))   All who are hungry   134

((O))   In the beginning   134

Ascension Day   137

((O))   Opening and closing responses for Ascension Day   138

We know you and we do not know you   138

What are you doing here?   138

In the name of the Maker   138

We go in hope   139

God of laughter and tears   139

✛   In a cloud   140

✞   A prayer for Ascension Day   140

✞   Ascension intercessions   142

✞   Let us celebrate   144

𝄞   Help us to see   146

Pentecost   147

((O))   Opening and closing responses for Pentecost Sunday   148

God speaks to us   148

God of fire and beauty   148

((O))   Opening responses for a Pentecost service   148

✛   The surprising thing about Pentecost   149
✟   A prayer for Pentecost   152
((◯))   An affirmation for Pentecost   153
₷   Fire songs   154
✟   When the day of Pentecost came   155
♫   Come, Holy Spirit   156
₷   On the great day of Pentecost   157
♥   Holy Spirit meditation   158
✟   The gift of Yourself – intercessions for Whitsunday   158
✟   Prayers of intercession for Pentecost   160
✟   Pentecost prayer   161
♥   A meditation for Pentecost   162
✟   Come among us   164
₷   Come, Holy Spirit   165
✟   God of fire   165
♫   Sudden from out the air   166

Holy Spirit   167

♫   On everyone who looks to God   168
₷   Mysterious God   169
✟   Free flowing Spirit   170
♫   O Holy Spirit   170
₷   God's whisper   171
₷   Visiting my nana   171
♫   Litany of the Spirit   172
♫   Like a wild bird (a baptismal hymn)   174
₷   Rejoice! O Daughter of Zion   175
₷   Walking with the Holy Spirit   176
♫   Lord God, whose Spirit drives us out   176

Saints' days   177

₷   Being remembered   178
♫   A hymn for St David's Day   179
₷   Saints alive (for Saint Beuno)   180
♫   Love is God's meaning: a liturgy to celebrate
    the feast day of Julian of Norwich, 8th May   181
♫   A place of refuge: a liturgy to celebrate
    the feast day of St Melangell, 27th May   185

Key to symbols	
✟	Prayer
₷	Reading
✛	Biblical reflection
♫	Liturgy
((◯))	Responses
♫	Song
✍	Story
📖	Sermon
🎭	Drama
🚲	Practical
♥	Meditation

☎   Gary   189
𝄞   Voyage – Pentecost, 563   192
♫   The pilgrim road   193
𝄞   Listen to their silence   194
𝄞   Brendan   195
♫   Their earthly journey closed   196
𝄞   Bede   198

Trinity   199
((◉))   Opening and closing responses for Trinity Sunday   200
    What is God like?   200
    Be strong and happy   200
    In the beginning, God the Maker   200
    In us God lives   201
    God the Maker   201
    By love and through the Maker   201
✟   A prayer for Trinity Sunday   202
♫   Audaciously and graciously   204
𝄞   Without you   205
✟   Transformation   206
𝄞   Alpha, Omega and Emmanuel in the inner city   207
📖   The Trinity as a circle   209
✟   Knowing her blessing   211
✟   Wayfaring   212

Environmental days   213
    Be Nice to Nettles Week   214
✟   *The docken leaf of your love*   214
🚲   *Picking nettles*   215
🚲   *Two recipes for nettle soup*   215, 216
🚲   *Nettle tea*   216
🚲   *Nettles growing in the garden*   217
🚲   *Compost*   217
🚲   *To deter mildew, blackflies and aphids on plants*   217
✟   A prayer for World Oceans Day   218
♨   Recycling – resources for a service of commitment   218

Joining Church   221

🝑   Getting the wean done   222
𝄞   It happened again yesterday   223
♫   Jesus risen from the grave   224
♫   Shot through and through with wonder   225
𝄞   Hungry and thirsty for justice   226
🝑   An Easter blessing   226
🝑   Big Tommy's confirmation   228

Making and keeping promises   231

✝   Two ordination prayers: 232
          Ordination   232
          True beauty   232
✝   Three prayers of consecration: 233
          This year's journeying   233
          Here is my life   234
          For the life of your world   235
♫   See, it is done   236
𝄞   Christ!   237
✝   Devoted as I am   238

Being Church   239

✝   Gathering   240
🝑   Being Church   240
♫   Doubt and faith   242
♫   Song of the Lord's reviving (after Ezekiel 37)   243
𝄞   Pilgrimage home   244
♫   Not just to prayer and worship we're committed   245
✝   Living, learning and laughing together   246
𝄞   Another rejection   246
🝑   Someone like me (A story from Iona)   247
✝   We offer this building   248
𝄞   Grapes   250
𝄞   Embarrassed   250
𝄞   Appearances   251

Key to symbols	
✝	Prayer
𝄞	Reading
✛	Biblical reflection
🝑	Liturgy
((•))	Responses
♫	Song
🝑	Story
📖	Sermon
🎭	Drama
🚲	Practical
♥	Meditation

I am   253

♫   Alleluia   254

𝄞   Gates and bread   255

𝄞   I am the Bread   256

♫   The Bread of the Lord   257

♫   Water of life   258

♫   I am the vine   260

𝄞   This door?   260

♫   Hymn based on the I am sayings of Jesus   262

✝   Prayers based on the I am sayings of Jesus   263

✍   A dismissal   264

Eucharist, feasting and celebration   265

♫   Take, eat, this is my body   266

✍   The feast of life: a service of commitment (Iona Abbey, 1998)   266

𝄞   A foretaste of the heavenly banquet   272

𝄞   The bread and cup pass me by   273

♫   Bread   274

♫   We're longing for a different world   276

🐌   Potter's House Eucharist   277

♫   And are the bread and wine your body, Lord?   279

𝄞   Birthday celebration   280

𝄞   At the gates   281

𝄞   The Body of Christ   281

♥   Dancing with the Creator   282

𝄞   The cup   284

Community   285

♫   Glory to God in the High Street   286

🐌   The Church in the community (A story from the Gorbals)   287

𝄞   Vision   288

🐌   Abbott and Costello Meet The Mummy   289

𝄞   The touch of God   295

✝   During a power cut   295

✝   The chance to make a difference   296

🐌   Esme and Peter   296

🎜 Who am I to get in your way, my God?   299
♫ Welcome each other   300
🖎 Gerry   300
♫ The long loneliness   304
♕ Fair exchange   306

Creation and new life   309

🎜 Fingerprints   310
✟ Life on Iona after winter   310
♥ New life (a meditation)   311
((◎)) Promise of spring   312
♫ A hymn of thanksgiving for lambing   313
🎜 Creation   314
🎜 Daffodil   314
✟ May God's springtime surge through me   315
🎜 Sun song (for a rainy day)   316
✟ A prayer on a wet day   316
🎜 It all has to do with   317
🎜 Rogation Day   318
✟ Fire and bread   320

🎭 The Bible in about an hour   321

Songs and prayers for the journey   337

♫ In the Kingdom's ventures   338
🎜 Beyond Easter   339
✟ God of the elements   339
✟ In you I love and glory   340
✟ Sweet Jesus   340
✟ Lead us and bless us   341
♫ Risen Lord (A heart for the simple things)   342

Key to symbols	
✟	Prayer
🎜	Reading
✥	Biblical reflection
♕	Liturgy
((◎))	Responses
♫	Song
🖎	Story
📖	Sermon
🎭	Drama
🚲	Practical
♥	Meditation

For Robin and Sue,
with shared memories of an open fire
and crumpets and blackcurrant jam

INTRODUCTION

Fire and Bread is a resource book which covers the period from Easter Sunday to Trinity Sunday, often referred to as Eastertide.

It is a companion volume to *Eggs and Ashes: Practical & Liturgical resources for Lent and Holy Week, Candles & Conifers: Resources for All Saints' and Advent*, and *Hay & Stardust: Resources for Christmas to Candlemas*, all published by Wild Goose.

Whilst a number of complete liturgies are included, most of the material in this book consists of the stuff that liturgies are made of: stories, songs, prayers, ceremonies, responses, poems, biblical reflections and sermons. Also included is a play entitled 'The Bible in about an hour'! – with the potential for a cast of hundreds, or a handful, and vast scope for innovative scenery.

My grateful thanks to all contributors for their rich and varied material which I have been privileged to edit – it's been a pleasure and a delight. If you have written something in a workshop on Iona and recognise your unnamed work, please let me know who you are so that your work can be acknowledged.

Thanks are also due, as always, to the Wild Goose Publications team – to Sandra Kramer, Jane Darroch-Riley, Alex O'Neill, Tri Boi Ta and Lorna Rae, for their encouragement, professionalism and support; and particularly to Neil Paynter, for whose cheery emails and attention to detail I am hugely grateful. Thanks also to Scott Riley for his artwork.

Risen Christ,
we are full of questions,
and you are full of life.

Break open in us,
this Easter,
your justice,
your tears,
and your joy.

Ruth Burgess
Advent 2006

EASTER DAY

OPENING AND CLOSING RESPONSES FOR EASTER DAY

Acts 10:34:37–43; Ps 118; 1 Cor 5:6–8; Jn 20:1–9

Give thanks that God is good
LET US CELEBRATE THE FEAST

Give thanks that Jesus is risen
LET US CELEBRATE THE FEAST

Give thanks that we are alive
LET US CELEBRATE THE FEAST

> Glory to God
> JESUS IS RISEN. ALLELUIA!
>
> Glory to God
> WHAT MORE CAN WE SAY?!
>
> Glory to God
> YOUR LIFE IS OUR STORY
>
> Glory to God
> YOUR LOVE IS OUR WAY

Ruth Burgess

EASTER GLORY FILLS THE HEAVEN

(Tune: Abbot's Leigh)

Easter glory fills the heaven,
Easter light pervades the earth,
now the Son, his triumph given,
brings his promise of new birth.
By his awesome act of giving,
sin and death are put to flight,
hope and life invade our living,
new created by his light.

On that wondrous Easter morning,
to the women at the tomb,
just as day was at its dawning,

Lord, you came and banished gloom.
Open now our hearts for hearing
your own living word of peace,
peace that conquers all our fearing:
our renewal, our release.

Come, as round the table, meeting,
we would be your people here,
taking, breaking, sharing, eating;
in the bread and wine draw near.
In our serving and forgiving
we would be your people true.
May we know, in all our living,
you in us, our life in you.

Lord of loving, Lord of glory,
through your giving, through your pain,
this the fullness of your story,
earth herself is born again.
Serving you through all your creatures,
great or small, or high or low,
we will then discern your features;
know your Resurrection, now.

Leith Fisher

AN EASTER COMMUNION

Invitation

Come to this table
where the living Christ
offers us bread broken
for our journeying
and wine poured out
for our tears.

Share together in this meal
where loss finds comfort in promise
and despair is transformed into hope.

Whoever you are, whatever you bring,

hear the risen Christ call your name;
and accept God's invitation to new life.

Prayer of thanksgiving

Easter God,
we bring you our praise and our thanks.
You take the pain of our Good Fridays,
the watching of suffering and the waiting for death,
and transform our helplessness
into the fragile beginnings of hope.
You take the bleakness of our Easter Saturdays,
the weariness of defeat and desolation,
and transform our despair
into the will and courage to go on.
You take the grieving of Easter Sunday morning,
the fearful approach to the tomb,
and transform our bewilderment
into the breathless excitement of new life.

And so, with Mary and the disciples,
with all who have wept and been comforted,
with all who have mourned and found hope,
we sing your Easter praises:

A sung hallelujah

So, God of loss and love,
we give you thanks for these signs
of broken bread and poured-out wine.
May they speak to us
of the everyday made holy,
of oppression turned to freedom and justice,
of new life dancing in our veins.
May we not cling to what is past,
but answer joyfully to the calling of our names –
to live your risen life
in the world you have made new. Amen

Post-Communion prayer

Easter God,
you have met us in bread and wine,
and surprised us with your joy.
Send us out into the world
dancing with delight
and with hallelujahs
ringing in our hearts,
to share your justice and your praise.
Amen

Jan Berry

ON THOSE TIMES

(An Easter confession)

Let us open our lives to God and ask for his forgiveness and grace:

On those times when we have kept your resurrection as a past event
    rather than a present encounter:
Lord, have mercy.
LORD, HAVE MERCY.

On those times when we have been blind to your presence:
Lord, have mercy.
LORD, HAVE MERCY.

On those times when we have failed to live as those who have risen with Christ:
Lord, have mercy.
LORD, HAVE MERCY.

To all who turn to him, Christ says, 'Your sins are forgiven.'
He also says, 'Come, follow me.'
THANKS BE TO GOD. AMEN

David Hamflett

A NEW DAY

A new day dawns.
February frosts cling
as snowdrops raise their heads in triumph.

A new day dawns.
Lent begins;
birds sing, waiting for a promise of spring.

A new day dawns.
Proud primulas peek
as expectant buds swell in stillness.

A new day dawns.
In a garden far away
your passion unfolds.

A new day dawns.
New life begins
through crowns of golden daffodils.

A new day dawns.
A promise kept, a gift for all.

On Easter Day I come with life,
life to the full.
Take. Begin. Alleluia.

Sarah Pascoe

LORD OF LIFE AND RESURRECTION

(Tune: Bethany)

Lord of Life and Resurrection,
in a graveyard damp with dew,
you bequeathed God's plan and pattern
to a weak and frightened few.
And the message of their story
still today remains the same:
Lives surrendered to God's purpose
open up His Kingdom's reign!

So I set my life before you –
all its passion, joy and pain,
contradictions, strength and weakness –
to receive your touch again.
Breathe your Spirit through its textures,
shape its patterns, mend its wrong;
so my dying and my living
may release your Kingdom's song.

Take my feet and lead them outward
from the safety I would choose,
to those hard and unknown places
where you want to bring Good News.
Take my hands and through their actions
fight injustice, bring release;
by their making and their mending
show your Kingdom's hope and peace.

Take my heart and pierce its armour
that true loving may be born,
and my life become a shelter
for those weary, hurt and worn.
Take my mind and quicken insight,
sharpen questions, so I can –
through a growing understanding –
help unfold your Kingdom's plan.

Thus in journey and in action
may I make your Presence real;
all my loving and my thinking
your true patterning reveal.
May the life which here I offer
make your Kingdom plain to see;
then what started in the graveyard
will continue on through me.

Pat Bennett

VERY EARLY IN THE MORNING

Opening responses:

This is the day:
WHEN TEARS ARE WIPED AWAY,
SHATTERED HEARTS ARE MENDED,
FEARS ARE REPLACED WITH JOY.

This is the day:
WHEN THE LORD ROLLS AWAY THE STONE OF FEAR,
THROWS OFF DEATH'S CLOTHES,
GOES AHEAD OF US INTO GOD'S FUTURE.

This is the day the Lord has made:
DEATH HAS NO FEAR FOR US,
SIN HAS LOST ITS POWER OVER US,
GOD OPENS THE TOMBS OF OUR HEARTS
TO FILL US WITH LIFE.

This is the day – Easter Day!
CHRIST IS RISEN!
HALLELUJAH!

Prayer of approach

Astounding God,
very early on that first day
you caught chaos unawares:

planting grace in a garden,
setting love loose on creation,
flinging joy into the air.

Jesus, Sun of Justice,
very early on that first day
you staggered sin,
throwing its weight off the world;
you confounded death,
leaving it alone in the grave;
you opened the gates of the kingdom,
so all could follow you into life.

Scarred Spirit,
very early on this first day of the week,
while we were washing sleep from our eyes
and trying to make sense of our lives,
you sang glad songs to us,
rolling away fears from our hearts
so we can see the Risen Lord.

God in Community, Holy and One,
very early on this first day of the week,
we lift our prayers to you,
using the words that Jesus taught us:

The Lord's prayer

Call to reconciliation:

Very early in the morning,
God created all that is good and beautiful.
Very early in the morning,
a mother placed her newborn in a manger.
Very early in the morning,
the good news that Jesus was risen and alive in their midst
    was shared with frightened friends.

Let us confess the fears we bring this morning ...

Silent prayers may be offered.

Prayer of confession

Emptier of tombs,
on this morning of hallelujahs,
we must confess how human we are.
We haven't done any great evil,
but we have failed to do good when we had the chance.
We easily accept the witness of the angel in the tomb,
but find it difficult to share this good news with our friends and neighbours.

Dazzling God,
bring us to life.
Where we are tired and stressed,
give us the energy to serve your creation;
transform our hardened hearts into fountains of grace;
forgive us for all the damage we have done –
and fill us with the joy of your Spirit.

Assurance of pardon:

God, our Creator, gives us new life;
Christ, our Redeemer, prepares a table for us;
The Holy Spirit, our Joy, calls us to service.
This is the good news:
The tomb is empty, sin is powerless, death is defeated for ever.
ON THIS VERY FIRST DAY,
AND EVERY DAY,
WE WALK AS GOD'S PEOPLE –
FORGIVEN AND MADE WHOLE.
THANKS BE TO GOD. AMEN

Prayer of thanksgiving:

The God of every morning be with you.
AND ALSO WITH YOU.
People of Easter morning, lift up your hearts!
WE LIFT THEM TO THE ONE
WHO HAS RAISED JESUS FROM THE GRAVE.
People of Easter's joy, give thanks to the One who raises us to new life.
WE SING OUR HALLELUJAHS TO THE GOD OF EVERLASTING LOVE.

Redeemer of the lost,
on this day of joy and hope,
we sing our praises to you.

Very early in the morning,
your Word shattered the silence of chaos,
and grace flowed forth like a river.
You reached down
and gathered up the dust of creation,
forming us into your image
and breathing life into us.
Yet the day came
when we chose to turn from you,
believing our wisdom was superior
to your will for us.
You sent us the prophets
to speak of your gracious hope,
but we refused to listen.
When you could have let us remain
in the clutches of sin and death,
you sent Jesus to be one of us,
so we could come home to you.

Therefore, we join our voices this morning
with those who stood at the empty tomb –
as well as with those of every place and time –
singing our Easter joy to you:

Sanctus (sung)

Holy are you, God of every day,
and blessed is Jesus Christ,
Bright Morning Star.

Creator of all that is good,
he entered the shadows of hell
to lead us into hope's light.

Beloved of your heart,
he embraced our sin
so we could be forgiven.

Glory beyond imagination,
he welcomed death
so we could enter life eternal.

Even as we believe
what we may not understand,
we trust that mystery we call faith.

Memorial acclamation

Resurrecting God,
it is here at this table
that we are fed by your love.
As you pour out your Spirit
upon the bread and the cup,
fill us with the spirit of Jesus,
so we may go forth to be your people.
Feed us with the Bread of Heaven,
so we can fill the hunger of the world.
Touch our lips with salvation's cup,
so we can proclaim the good news
of this day to everyone we meet.

And when the morning comes
when we are united with all the saints
gathered around heaven's table,
we will lift our voices to you,
God in Community, Holy and One,
for ever and ever. Amen

Communion follows

Thom M. Shuman

LORD, WE HAVE SEEN YOU WALKING

Words: Carol Dixon
Tune: 'Have you not seen my lady', G.F. Handel

1. Lord, we have seen you walk-ing the gar-den at dew-y dawn-ing;
Lord, we have heard you talk-ing as bird-songs greet the morn-ing; and,
Lord, we have met you liv-ing where once we__ thought you__ dead;
and we re-joice to find you__ bless-ing the bro-ken bread.

2. Lord, we have seen you caring
   for those who were filled with sorrow;
   Lord, we have heard you sharing
   your hope for a new tomorrow;
   and, Lord, we have felt you filling
   our lives with your love divine –
   and we receive your new life
   as we share bread and wine.

AMONG THE CHILDREN

(Easter Sunday sermon, Iona Abbey, 2006)

Bible reading: John 20:1–9

This morning we are very glad to have so many children here with us in the Abbey. And I'd like to invite the children to come down and join me here in the crossing …

I hope you're all having a good holiday here on Iona: some staying in the Abbey, some in the MacLeod Centre, some elsewhere on the island.

In the story we've just heard from the Bible, when a very good friend of Jesus, called Mary, went to where he was buried, because she was sad, she found that he wasn't there. *How do you think she must have felt?* …

'But there were two messengers there, and they said to her: "Why are you looking for the living among the dead? He isn't here. He's alive, and he's just gone on ahead of you to Galilee. Go and look for him there!"' *How do you think Mary must have felt then? … Who knows what Galilee was?* …

Galilee was the place Jesus came from, and most of his best friends came from there too. So really, the messengers were saying: He's gone home ahead of you. Go and look for him among people who are alive.

My friend Ruth and I were talking about this story, and we were wondering: Where could people look for Jesus today? So I was wondering: *Where do **you** think we might find Jesus now, in our world?* …

These are really good answers. And I thought you might like to hear some of the answers that Ruth and I came up with.

Among the children

First of all, we thought we could look for Jesus among the children, because Jesus really loved children, and liked to meet them and play with them, and didn't mind when they made a noise in church. He got very cross when people hurt children; and he made a lot of children who were sick or sad feel better … like this girl:

The Syrophoenician woman's daughter's story

Something happened to me when I was little.
My mum told me that a man called Jesus had healed me.
No one knew what was wrong with me.
She'd been desperate –
and when my mum's desperate she doesn't take no for an answer.

She'd heard that a healer called Jesus was in the district, and she'd gone to him –
given his disciples a hard time until she got to see him face to face;
and when she saw him, they argued –
that's something my mum is good at –
lots of eye contact and passion.
They both gave as good as they got.
Mum said he really enjoyed it –
it was the kind of conversation that he rarely got to get –
and he got the last word:
he healed me.

My mum told me last week that she'd heard he'd been killed.
She was sad. She cried ...
But this morning she was laughing:
There was a rumour going round that he'd had the last word to beat all last words –
he'd come back from the dead, and he'd been seen going home to Galilee.

I reckon anyone who can win an argument with my mum
must be someone quite amazing.
Maybe one day I'll get to meet him.

So Ruth and I think that you can find Jesus with children, having fun with them, listening to them, caring about them when they're ill – and especially with children who have hard lives, like children who live in places where there's war or violence, or children who get picked on at school, or children who have no grown-ups to look after them, and are hungry or cold.

Among the poor

And then Ruth and I thought that we could find Jesus among people who are poor, especially with the ones who have no one to help them, or who can't get jobs and don't have enough money to live on. And in a lot of countries that means they have to become beggars, like this man:

Blind Bartimaeus's story

I followed Jesus.
I wanted to.
There was no point me sitting at the side of the road in Jericho any more.
I could see.
Jesus had healed me.

I could see where I was going.
I could choose for myself what I wanted to do.

I followed him for a week.
I saw him ride into Jerusalem –
his long legs dangling over the back of that wee donkey.
I enjoyed feeling safe and confident in a crowd.
I listened to him when he told stories.
I saw how his enemies were never far away.
I was there when he carried his cross through the streets on the way to the crucifixion.
I almost wished then I couldn't see what was happening –
so much sadness in his eyes, so much pain.
I saw the tomb where they put his body – my eyes filled up with tears.

Eventually I went home to Jericho.
Everything had changed for me.
People weren't sure how to talk to me.
I didn't need to beg any longer – but I didn't have any other trade.
I didn't need anyone to guide me around.
I could look after myself.
It was scarey and exciting at the same time.

And it's still like that:
every day I see something new,
every day I'm learning how to be independent –
how to cook, how to fish –
and I'm learning how to read;
and there's this woman I often see in the marketplace;
she smiles at me, and I smile back.
It feels good.

So we think that you can still find Jesus walking along with people who are poor, chatting away to them, helping them to be brave enough to go on, and getting angry when countries and governments and businesses act as if their profits are more important than people.

Among outsiders and people who are discriminated against

And then Ruth and I thought that we'd very likely find Jesus with people who get treated unfairly, who don't get an equal say, and with people who feel that they don't belong. Jesus met a lot of people like that; sometimes they were foreigners or outsiders; maybe they had a different religion or spoke differently. Sometimes other people disapproved of them and were always going: 'Tut tut, she's a bad person …' – as if we didn't all do bad things sometimes. Like this woman:

The Samaritan woman's story

I was nervous enough when I saw him at the well. I always went at noon, when the heat is fiercest, because I knew that no one else went then.

It was best to go alone. That way, there were none of my own people there, to snigger and sneer, or to bump into me on purpose so I spilled my water, because I've been with a lot of men. They don't like it that I won't go grovelling to them, so they can feel superior.

And there's no one from his people, who simply don't see me because I'm a Samaritan, beneath their notice. They think we're heathens who don't know anything about God, and haven't been chosen. But I know that I'm neither evil nor stupid. I'm just a woman on her own, trying to get by in a man's world.

But this man seemed to live in a *different* world. He drank from my bowl. We talked for a long time, proper talk, as he would to a man. He seemed to know all about me. And then he told me this important thing, something you could only tell somebody you trusted.

Well, I had to tell people. I knew they might laugh at me, and it was hard to break my silence. But what I had to tell them was so immense that, out of curiosity, they came to hear him for themselves. And they were convinced too.

Now I'm not known as *that bad woman*. Now I'm known as the messenger, the woman who brought them the good news.

Well, even today, even in this country, there are still a lot of people who don't get treated equally. People don't listen to them, and are unkind to them, even though they might have had a very bad time. They can feel really lonely and afraid. So we definitely think you would find Jesus making friends with them, taking them seriously, making them feel welcome and at home – and telling everybody else to do the same.

Among people who share

One of the things that Jesus talked about a lot was how important it is to share things, especially when some people have a lot and some people have hardly anything. He thought that was a good thing to do, partly so that then everyone would have enough but also because it's a very good feeling when everyone can enjoy things together. A feeling this boy had:

The story of the boy with the loaves and fishes

I like Jesus.
I met him once.
I'd gone with my friend's family to listen to him telling stories
    on the other side of the lake.
My mum had packed me a picnic.

When it came to teatime,
Jesus stopped talking to us, and said something quietly to his friends.
They looked worried.
I knew Andrew. He's from our village.
I heard him say something about people being hungry.
He was near me, and I pulled his sleeve;
I told him that mum had packed me a big picnic,
and if anyone was hungry, they could share it with me.
The man with Andrew heard me, but ignored me –
grown-ups are like that sometimes; they're rude –
but Andrew grabbed my hand and took me to Jesus and told him what I'd said.
Jesus took my picnic –
the bread my mum had baked, the fish she'd bought down the market –
and you know what happened next?
Jesus shared my picnic with everyone.

I like Jesus.
He listens to what people say.
He listens to children.
He cares about hungry people.
He made me feel happy that I could help him.

So Ruth and I thought that you could find Jesus where people share good things – like meals, laughter and singing, but also things like their time, their money, their problems

… By sharing things like time and money we can see what it might be like to live in a world where no one has to go to bed hungry, or without the medicine they need, or not being able to read. We think that would be really something!

Among people who are sad

And last of all, we think that we could find Jesus beside people who are sad. Jesus didn't always stop people being sad. (Sometimes that's important, and it would be very strange if you weren't sad when someone you love has died or gone away, or when something very difficult has happened to them.) But he would keep them company when they felt particularly low; and he would remind them that, even though the person had gone away, the love was still there. And he would ask them to do something for him that gave them a reason to look forward and not just back. Like this woman:

Mary's story

I saw angels this morning, in the garden.

Angels, asking me why I was crying –
do angels understand sadness?
Do angels know what it's like to lose someone you've loved,
to not know where they've gone?

Through my tears, I saw a man standing there in the distance.
I thought he was the gardener.
I asked him if he'd moved the body of Jesus
and he spoke to me.
He called me by name:
'Mary.'
I turned to him … I answered him:
'Teacher.'
Through the ache of my tears, I felt wonder and joy.
I wanted that moment to last for ever,
but he gave me a job to do.
He sent me to tell the disciples what was happening.

I saw angels this morning …
angels and Jesus.

Now I know something of their glory and joy.

These are some of the places that Ruth and I think we might find Jesus today. We might not recognise him; he might even look like someone we know. But he'd be there. And we think that if anyone's having a hard time finding Jesus, these are good places to start.

Prayer (Looking in the wrong places)

Lord Jesus,
we are always looking for you in the wrong places;
among the good and respectable people,
when we should know you are to be found
with the poor and disreputable and outcast.

Lord Jesus,
we are always looking for you in the wrong places,
at a safe distance,
but you come so close to us,
nearer to us than breathing.

We look for you in churchy things,
but we are more likely to find you
among the pots and pans,
or around the kitchen table ...

We look for you in buildings,
but you walked crowded streets,
and shorelines
and mountains ...

Even now, even after Easter,
still we insist on trying to find you among the tombstones;
among long-dead dogmas,
in old, decaying fears and hurts,
in the guilts and resentments we inhabit like a coffin.

But the angel said:
Why do you look for him among the dead?
He is not here!

Lord Jesus, help us to lay down the graveclothes,
roll away the stone
and come out into life,
here and now.

We will find you,
among the living,
ahead of us, going to the Galilee we seek.
You have wrestled death to the ground,
and now there is nowhere we can go,
no darkness we can enter,
which is not God-encompassed.

Ruth Burgess and Kathy Galloway

RISEN, GLORIOUS CHRIST

Risen, glorious Christ,
we join with all your people
in heaven and on earth
to greet you,
and to celebrate
the victory you have won.

And what a victory!

Beneath you, defeated,
lie all humanity's ancient foes:
pride, self-sufficiency, status,
security, even death.
By your triumph on the Cross
you have put back in their proper place
those things we have come to rely on
for life itself:
friends, health, family,
occupation, achievement, success.
Lifted high on the Cross,
you hold up before us
the ultimate power of love;
risen glorious from the tomb,
you stand beside us now,
companion, brother, servant ...
and living God.
What can we do now but worship,
and praise, and seek to follow?

Master, for us you know full well
the strife is not over,
nor is the battle done.
Even as we celebrate
the completeness of your triumph
still we seek from you
succour and strength
for our lesser conflicts,
day by day.

If, in our warfare
against all that would dehumanise
and defile your creation,
we forget your way of waging battle –
forget to use your weapons
of faith
and hope
and unconditional love –
forgive us, we pray.

John Harvey

WE THOUGHT WE HAD HEARD IT ALL

(Lord, have mercy on us)

We thought we had heard it all,
dear God; we thought we knew.
The Bible stories; the words of our faith;
the rules for living
and the way to heaven;
we thought, dear God, we knew!
But here,
before the mystery again
of a grave that is empty
when it should have been filled
with a decaying corpse,
we know now,
that we know nothing at all.
LORD, HAVE MERCY ON US.

We thought we had heard it all,
dear God; we thought we knew.
The great stories of the Church;
the ebb and flow of the faith;
our place in the scheme of things;
we thought, dear God, we knew!
But here,
before the mystery again

of death defeated,
of broken folk made whole,
and mighty powers quite broken,
we know now,
that we know nothing at all.
LORD, HAVE MERCY ON US.

We thought we had heard it all,
dear God; we thought we knew.
The way of the world;
the powers that be and
the powers that would be;
the ebb and flow of armies
and international finance;
the endless tide of refugees
and the awfulness of hate;
we thought, dear God, we knew!
But here,
before the mystery again
of a word of love
in a quiet garden,
and the promise, suddenly,
of a new order of creation
in place of the old, tired, familiar scene,
we know now,
that we know nothing at all.
LORD, HAVE MERCY ON US.

John Harvey

RISEN CHRISTA

In the women who keep vigil for the dead and disappeared,
risking all to bring their offerings of defiance
and keep dangerous memories alive,
Christ is risen.
SHE IS RISEN INDEED.
ALLELUIA!

In the women whose courage rolls back the stone,
whose strength bears the weight of hunger, AIDS and debt
to find liberation in the struggle,
Christ is risen.
SHE IS RISEN INDEED.
ALLELUIA!

In the women who walk the road of uncovering abuse,
staying with the pain of violence until the recognition
of the beauty of God's image within,
Christ is risen.
SHE IS RISEN INDEED.
ALLELUIA!

In the women who raise their voices in protest for peace,
marching on the streets and weaving ribbons into wire
to speak reconciliation in a hostile world,
Christ is risen.
SHE IS RISEN INDEED.
ALLELUIA!

In the women refusing to be silenced by male authority,
flouting convention and tradition to tell their stories,
bringing new life through word and wisdom,
Christ is risen.
SHE IS RISEN INDEED.
ALLELUIA!

Jan Berry

FOR IT IS BY YOUR LOVE

Text: based on words by Thomas Traherne
Music: da Noust

Gently
Capo 3

For it is by your love that you en-joy all my de-lights, and are de-light-ful to me, Joy of my heart.

last time to Coda

VERSE

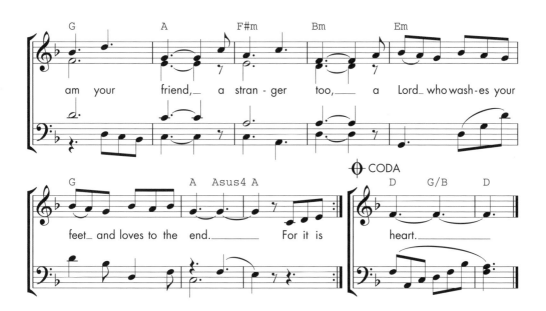

am   your   friend,_   a   stran - ger   too,_   a   Lord_ who wash - es your

feet_ and loves to the   end._   For it is   heart._

CODA

2. Can you not hear
    me summon you
    to leave your tomb at the call
    of covenant love.

RESURRECTION, LAUGHTER AND NEW LIFE

FOR NOW I AM MAKING YOU HEAR NEW THINGS

Text: based on Isaiah 48:6–8
Music: da Noust

For now I am mak-ing you hear new things, hid-den to you, as yet un-known; cre - a - ted just now, right at this mo -ment; of them you've heard no - thing till now, so you can - not say: 'Oh___ yes, I knew all this.' And I___ will bring, am bring-ing to flo - wer, all that heals you, all you de - sire; al - le - lu - ia, a - men, a - men.___

LITURGY FOR HOLY HUMOUR SUNDAY

Introduction

If churches wanted to declare a 'day off' from worship, most would probably choose the second Sunday of Easter. After the 'highs' of Easter Day, with its marvellous music, powerful preaching, sanctuaries overflowing with folks in Easter finery, the next Sunday is one of tired preachers, exhausted choirs and diminished attendance.

One way of fighting the 'lows' is to celebrate this day as Holy Humour/Hilarity Sunday. Holy Humour Sunday is a tradition dating back to the 1200s; it recognises that, while worship is a serious business, it should never be without laughter and joy.

In my church, folks come to the Holy Humour Sunday service wearing outlandish clothes and silly hats – we even had a mime in the congregation this year. I tell a lot of jokes, as well as stress the value of laughter for physical and spiritual health. This year we did a 'reverse offering', in which we passed around a basket of prescription bottles which contained jokes for folks to 'take once a day'.

Call to laughter

A: This is the time to rejoice!
ALL: WHAT BETTER TIME THAN NOW?!

A: This is the day to laugh: What did the pastor say to the people?
Pastor: Lettuce pray! *(while juggling two – or three! – lettuces).*

A: How many choir directors does it take to change a light bulb?
Choir: No one knows – because no one ever watches the director!

A: How many Presbyterians does it take to change a light bulb?
ALL: CHANGE? PRESBYTERIANS DON'T BELIEVE IN CHANGE!

A: What's the greatest joke ever?
ALL: THE ONE GOD PLAYED ON DEATH ON EASTER MORNING!

Prayer

Imaginative God,
you smiled and the sun burst
through the shadows of chaos;
you laughed,
and all that is good and beautiful
was given shape by you;

you chuckled,
and the platypus splashed
in creation's fountain.

Laughing Jesus,
snickering at the feeble attempts
of the Evil One,
you showed us
how to resist temptation;
giggling at sin's desperate desire
to hold on to us,
you released us by your love;
howling with laughter
at death's foolish belief
that the tomb could hold you,
you burst forth into the kingdom
as the stars pealed with joy.

Spirit of Easter,
as you fill us with new life,
may we delight in sharing it with others;
as you tell us the good news
which can never be taken from us,
may we rejoice in offering it
to the broken, the sad, the lonely;
as you tickle us with grace,
may we give it away
with laughter on our lips
and joy in our hearts.

God in Community, Holy and One,
our hearts overflow with wonder
as we say together the prayer that Jesus taught us:

The Lord's prayer

Call to reconciliation

None of us likes to look foolish. But which is sillier: chasing after the world and all its gaudy trinkets which flatter our souls, or being a 'fool for Christ', imitating him in service to others, offering ourselves in love and joy to the world? Let us admit to God the foolish choices we make each and every day ...

Silent prayers may be offered.

Prayer of confession

Amused God,
you know better than we do what important people we believe we are.
Believing we have to be serious all the time,
we miss out on the joy of your creation.
Choosing to feast on the pain of the world,
we skip the picnic offered in paradise.
Clinging to the despair which is our best friend,
we ignore Jesus who can bring us home to your heart.

FORGIVE US, HEART OF JOY,
AND MAKE US OPEN TO THE STARTLING,
AND UPSIDE DOWN,
WAYS IN WHICH YOU WORK.
FILL US WITH EASTER'S LAUGHTER;
FILL US WITH YOUR HEALING JOY;
FILL US WITH THE LOVE POURED INTO US
THROUGH JESUS CHRIST, OUR LORD AND SAVIOUR.

Assurance of pardon

The gospels tell us over and over again
of the joy which comes to us through Christ.
When Jesus was around, lives were changed:
the sick were healed, the sorrowful began to laugh.
The good news is that this joy is now given to us.

THROUGH THE HOLY SPIRIT,
WE ARE GIFTED WITH JOY.
WE ARE SENT FORTH TO BRING GOOD NEWS TO THE OPPRESSED,
TO BRING HEALING TO THE BROKEN,
TO ANOINT EVERYONE WITH THE OIL OF GLADNESS.
THANKS BE TO GOD, WE ARE FORGIVEN. AMEN

Thom M. Shuman

NEWNESS OF LIFE

When the bleak coldness of winter is warmed by the spring air,
and new shoots push through soil and buds open to the sun:
WE CELEBRATE NEWNESS OF LIFE
AND DANCE IN A CIRCLE OF JOY.

When weariness and withdrawal have rested body and spirit
and energy flows again in a spontaneous, unforced rhythm:
WE CELEBRATE NEWNESS OF LIFE
AND DANCE IN A CIRCLE OF JOY.

When the heaviness of grief and anger is lifted by hope,
and the tears shed in pain glisten like sparkling water:
WE CELEBRATE NEWNESS OF LIFE
AND DANCE IN A CIRCLE OF JOY.

When defeat and despair are transformed by the power of faith,
and from the ruins of our dreams new visions grow:
WE CELEBRATE NEWNESS OF LIFE
AND DANCE IN A CIRCLE OF JOY.

Jan Berry

STORY SNAPSHOTS

These snapshots can be performed in any order.

Heard the news?

A: Heard the news?
B: What news?
A: News about Laz.
B: That's history, not news – Laz is dead – died last week.
C: Shame though, I liked Laz, he was always good for a laugh.

A: No, not *that* news about Laz.
B: What news then?
A: Laz isn't dead any longer – he's alive again.
B: Dead man walking! Who are you kidding?
C: You shouldn't joke about stuff like that – it's weird.

A: But it's true.

B: It can't be.

A: It is – this gadgee* called Jesus brought him back to life again.

B: Can't have.

C: I've heard of this Jesus – the word is he's OK.

A: This Jesus gadgee went into the graveyard ...

B: Go on ...

A: And he shouted out Laz's name.

B: And ...

A: And Laz came out of his grave. Coo, what a pong!*

B: Ghost was he – all white sheets and spooky?

A: No, he was alive I tell you – he was Laz – scared and shaken like – but he was walking and talking.

B: Rubbish!

C: I've never heard of anyone really coming back from the dead before.

A: Go and have a look through Mary and Martha's window if you don't believe me

B: Why should I?

A: Cos Laz is there – eating – talking – breathing.

B: No way!

C: Only one way to find out – let's go and have a look.

Ruth Burgess

*Gadgee – geezer, bloke
*'Coo, what a pong' – added by children from St Vincent's Primary School, Walker, Newcastle upon Tyne, who performed this piece.

Mary

Me, I'm Mary.
It's my brother that's dead.
My eyes are sore.
I can't stop crying.

Everything seems to happen to us.
Lazarus was only a child when our parents died –
first our father, then just months later our mother.
Martha and I brought him up.
It was a struggle.
Neighbours helped.
We survived.

When Lazarus got ill
we tried to get Jesus to come –
we sent him a message.
He loved Lazarus and
he could have healed him.

Losing mum and dad was hard
but losing a brother, this feels harder.

Lazarus is gone
and with him my reason for living.

Jesus is our friend.
He loves us.
Why wasn't he here
when we needed him most?

Thomas

I'm a disciple.
I follow Jesus.
I'm Thomas.

We're going to Bethany
where Mary and Martha live.
Jesus has had a message
that Lazarus, their brother, has died.

I think that we're walking into trouble – again.
Last time that we were in that area

the locals threatened to stone him.

Surely Jesus could send a message back
to tell them that we're sorry for their trouble.
He doesn't need to go in person – does he?

The graveyard superintendent

Open the grave!
You can't do that.
It's against the rules.
I know – I'm the graveyard superintendent.
The rules are there to protect us,
to keep things safe.

Imagine if everyone
went about opening graves.
The place would be stinking.
We'd all catch diseases.

There is a proper time and place to grieve.
And a proper way to do it.

So don't let your emotions
run away with you.

Lazarus is dead and buried.
Accept it.

Say your prayers,
and get on with living.

Jesus

Lazarus, Mary and Martha are my friends.
In their home I felt safe.
I belonged.
I'm Jesus.

What I did
shocked
amazed
angered
revealed.

Life will not be the same again
for Lazarus
for Martha
for Mary
or for me.

Sometimes to challenge the accepted order,
to bring about change,
you have to take risks.

What I did today exhausted me, cost me.

Love is like that,
and I love my friends.

Martha

I'm Martha, the practical one,
the one who, with Mary, brought up my brother.
I nursed him in his last illness
and organised his burial.
It's not that I wasn't grieving with my sister.
I just keep my feelings to myself.

We had sent for Jesus,
but for some reason –
maybe he didn't get the message in time –
he didn't come until it was all over.

He arrived later,
talked with me about resurrection,
wept with Mary –
and then brought Lazarus back from the dead!

It was amazing!
I still look at Lazarus sometimes
and wonder if I dreamed it.

Jesus – my friend – he's practical –
and sometimes a bit scarey.

The mourners

A: Well, what about that then?
B: It was very odd.
A: I'd only gone to pay my respects to the sisters –
B: Me too.
A: And I saw it all.
B: The whole thing.

A: I'd heard about this Jesus before – a teacher they say.
B: And a healer.
A: And there he was – weeping at the graveside.
B: Strange that, a man crying in public.
A: I heard someone say that he'd taken his time coming. If he'd come earlier
    he could have saved Lazarus.
B: But he'd come too late for that.
A: Much too late.

A: And then he told them to take the gravestone away.
B: The graveyard superintendent nearly had a fit.
A: He tried to stop it.
B: Imagine the stink – it can't have been hygienic!
A: And then Jesus prayed a bit.
B: And talked a bit.
A: And then he shouted: 'Lazarus come out!'
B: Scared the life out of me that did!
A: I thought he'd gone mad.
B: I saw something white coming out of the grave.
A: Mrs Tobias was screaming!
B: Mrs Nehemiah fainted!
A: And then Jesus told the people near it – to unwrap him.
B: And it was Lazarus.
A: And he was breathing.
B: A miracle!

A: The Romans won't like it
B: Who cares? All they ever do is put up the taxes.
A: And someone's bound to tell the Pharisees
B: They probably already have!
A: Ah well, I'd better be getting back home.
B: Me too – I'm dying to tell my sister what she's missed.

Lazarus

They tell me I was dead.

I remember being ill,
and I woke up
because someone was calling my name.
Lazarus.

When I tried to get up
there were strips of cloth
round my hands and feet
and a cloth over my face.
I was scared.

I tried to move towards the light
and someone said:
'Untie him.'
The first thing I saw
was Jesus, my friend,
and he'd been crying.

When I walk down the street
people still point at me,
even those who know me well.
They seem scared,
afraid to talk to me.
Even Martha and Mary seem to have changed;
it's as if they were still looking after me
like they did when I was a child.

I didn't ask for this to happen to me.
I don't want to be different.
I don't want to be avoided and tiptoed around.

I want to turn the clock back.
I want everything to be the same as before.

The Lazarus story – the official view

This time
he's gone too far!
Last night the Pharisees (of whom I am one)
and the chief priests

met with the Council (to which I aspire to belong)
and held an emergency meeting
under Standing Orders Number 24, part 3c –
senior officials only.
Single agenda item:
What shall we do about Jesus of Nazareth?

Discussion was fast and furious.
I was able to tell my eyewitness account of what happened at Bethany,
and it was duly minuted.
Very gratifying.

Outcome:
Decision made according to Standing Orders Number 26, part 2a:
The recent actions of Jesus of Nazareth constitute a danger to public order
and a threat to religious authority.
This man needs to be removed.
Plans to dispose of him will be formulated and executed
    at the earliest possible opportunity.
End of meeting.

Very satisfying!

Ruth Burgess

TILLIE

(from a longer story about working in a home for the elderly)

Playing bingo with a reserved air is Tillie.

One evening after Bingo, Tillie told us all about the heavenly trip she'd taken to Hawaii a few years ago with her son and daughter-in-law. Evenings on the balcony of the posh hotel overlooking the ocean; the refreshing, fragrant breeze; the feeling of the world slowing down, and the waves thrusting.

'God just lovely,' she sighed ... 'And the prostitutes,' she giggled.

'What?'

'Pardon, Tillie?

She'd surprised us. She had always given us the impression of being very prim and proper. Someone you'd be careful not to swear around – a homey quilt on her neat bed, walls covered in little birds singing sweetly on branches, embroidery in progress. Yet it seemed Tillie got a kick out of watching the girls down on the boulevard, down on the strip, fighting over territory, cars and Johns. 'Tugging and pulling at each other's hair some of them. Kicking each other in the shins!'

Tillie leaned across the fold-up table and confided that, one evening, when her son and his wife had gone out for a night on the town, she switched off the television and went down the elevator to the hotel bar. There Tillie laughed and drank creamy drinks with an elderly gentleman and after last orders seduced him up to her room.

'I lost my virginity that night,' she cackled. 'Well, not exactly – but it had been so long it seemed so!' Tillie leaned over the table farther, her voice a whisper, a mischievous glimmer in her old eyes. 'You know, it takes a long time to get those old ones up, this one anyway, but once they're up ... And I loved the thought of the kids walking in. It made it more exciting. I would have loved to see their faces.'

Bless her, I thought. Tillie could still enjoy life. She had not lost that art in this place.

Neil Paynter

THIS DAY

Make this day, Lord, a step closer to heaven.
This day, Lord, may I know myself loved and valued.
This day, Lord, may I notice the beauty around me, in things great and small.
This day, Lord, may I not miss the messages of joy, of peace, of hope that you send me.
This day, Lord, this day ... make the day of my resurrection.

Richard Sharples

GOD OF THE PURPLE ROBE

God of the purple robe,
of the traitor's cross;
God of the torn curtain,
of the wounds of time,

lead us to Easter Day,
your joy day,
turn-about time.

You are the dance in our eyes,
the smile in our hearts,
the blossom of our spring.

You are our wounds and our laughter,
light that splits open the sky,
love that astonishes.

Judy Dinnen

SHATTER THE BOX

Good Friday –
the altar is bare
tabernacle door flung open
red light out
all to symbolise
that I am not here ...

And yet I am here
in a wonderfully free way
not packaged
locked in a box
meeting you where you are
no rituals needed.

Why do you look for the living among the dead?
I am forever calling your name
Do you not recognise me?
Get up, walk out!
Find me in the next person you meet
Not on your knees.

Easter Sunday –
flowers
vestments
door locked
red light on
the symbol that I am back ...

And I cry out to you:
Set me free
that you too may be free.

Together let's shatter the box.

Julia Brown

On Good Friday, the tabernacle, the box in the church where the reserved sacrament is held, is traditionally left empty, with the door open.

QUESTION TIME

Students from Churchill Community College, Wallsend, took up a 'write a drama for Easter' challenge with Sheila Hamil a couple of years ago, and as a result of their discussion and a sharing of ideas, Sheila wrote this Resurrection drama, based on the BBC programme Question Time. This idea could be adapted.

Host:	Welcome to Question Time! I'm speaking to you from the auditorium at Churchill Community College, Wallsend.
	Our first guest on this week's panel of experts is Gaius Gallius, leader of the Roman guards responsible for the death of Jesus of Nazareth.
	Next, we have the mother of Jesus, Mary. I know she won't mind me mentioning that there was great fuss around at the time of the birth of her son – and many questions were asked about who the real father of her child was.
	Then we have Annas, an expert in Religious Affairs and a key member of the Pharisee Party.
	And finally we have Thomas, a disciple of Jesus, who, by his own admission, had many doubts about Jesus, but who is now a firm believer in the cause of Christianity.
	We have our first question from the floor. Please, go ahead.
Audience member:	Do the members of the panel think that Jesus was *really* raised from the dead?
Annas:	Jesus did not rise from the dead any more than you or I could. It was a trick! How can anyone possibly believe that that could happen? No, the truth is that he was not actually dead when he was put into the tomb – and the cool air revived him. Then he simply escaped.
Gaius:	No, I can't agree with that because I, personally, made sure he was dead before we took him down from the cross. One of my soldiers pierced his side with a spear, and blood and water suddenly flowed out – a sure sign of death. Anyhow, if he did revive himself in the tomb, how could he have moved that heavy stone by himself? And you forget, my men were there on duty.
Thomas:	And I actually saw him myself in the upper room ... I put my fingers in the holes in his hands and feet. He told me to, because I hadn't believed it was possible either!

Annas:	All right then, let's say there was a twin involved –
Mary:	I think I'd know if I'd given birth to two babies! You can ask the shepherds, the wise men from the east, the innkeeper and his wife – and my husband, if you don't believe me.
Annas:	OK, then there was a look-alike.
Thomas:	I tell you it was Jesus! He was alive! How could a 'look-alike' have had injuries like that and not been crippled or in agony?
Mary:	And I think I would know my own son!
Annas:	Well, there has to be a logical explanation … It's quite obvious to me then that the disciples came in the night, while the guards were asleep, and stole the body.
Gaius:	My soldiers don't fall asleep on the job! They'd be executed if they did.
Thomas:	Besides, the history books will one day show that many of us were actually put to death and tortured for our faith. Would we put ourselves through all that for a lie?
Mary:	*(to Annas and Gaius)* Have either of you hidden the body of my son?
Annas:	Don't be silly. If we had, we would produce the body as evidence, wouldn't we?
Gaius:	I'll say so!
Mary:	Well then, it makes you wonder, doesn't it?
Annas:	*(sounding desperate)* No, I realise now what happened. Those who claim to have seen Jesus must have been on drugs. They were just hallucinating! They only thought they saw him. Or it was a trick of the mind.
Thomas:	I wouldn't take drugs, that's not how I was brought up – and anyway lots of people saw him at different times. On one occasion five hundred people saw him at once. If they were on drugs or hallucinating, wouldn't everyone have seen different things?
Annas:	*(panicking)* All right, let me think! People don't just rise from the dead. I know … a thief took the body.
Thomas:	In that case the expensive linen cloth and the oils would have gone too.
Gaius:	And besides you still need to remember that my guards were on duty.

Host: Well, it appears that no satisfactory explanation can be given.

Gaius: Well, I said it then, and I'll say it now: perhaps this man really was the Son of God.

Annas: Oh, hold your tongue!

Gaius: *(literally holds his tongue and says:)* Don't you tell me what to say.

Host: OK, I think at this point we need to take a break. The situation's getting rather sticky.

Sheila Hamil and students from Churchill Community College

EASTER OFFERING

Lord,
as I contemplate your cross
I am drawn
not into intellectual understanding
but into the passionate reality
of your love.

So I offer you my wounds
not for resolution and healing
but to be held, with yours,
in your Body.

Lord,
as I am confined in the tomb
I am drawn
not into intellectual understanding
but into the relentless patience
of your waiting.

So I offer you my fallow time
not for resolution and release
but to be held, with yours,
until your moment.

Lord,
as I encounter you in the garden
I am drawn

not into intellectual understanding
but into the vibrant possibilities
of your resurrection.

Take my wounds and my waiting
and, in your rising,
liberate their potential.

That what is mortal
may be transformed
by Life.

Pat Bennett

THE INVITATION OF EASTER

And across our beautiful,
evolving world
another Easter dawns,
tenderly inviting us
to ponder upon
wider truths
and alternative visions.

Truths of both heart and mind
that find their roots
in the mystery and practicality
of God.

Basic truths
illumining
our often uncertain journeys –
allowing us
to reconnect with the
energies of Christ:

That life does come from death;
that hate is not the final word;
that the broken continue to sing with joy:
that the trees and the mountains clap their hands;
that forgiveness resides in the heart of the human condition;

that love, with its multiple faces, remains our companion.

So Christ is risen!
Risen again
in the midst of it all –
that in some amazing way
we too
may be a people of hope
who walk in the light,
imbued with the Spirit.

Peter Millar

HIDE AND SEEK

Sometimes we go looking for God
and sometimes we find God.

Far better to let God find us
since God is always looking.

The real art is in discerning
when God is right under your nose:

familiar yet surprising,
comforting yet unexpected.

No wonder Easter is life-changing!

Judith Jessop

TOWARDS FREEDOM

I feel so much fear
You give me your hug
I feel so much anger
You give me your understanding
I feel so much bitterness
You give me your protection
I feel so much resentment
You give me your tenderness

I feel so much hate
You give me your love

I find you
You give me myself.

Julia Brown

PRAYERS OF THE HEART

Risen Christ,
hear the prayer of my heart
not the dull confusion of my mind.
Hear the tears I will not shed,
the grief I hide in busyness,
and bring your resurrection love
weaving new life.

Risen Christ,
hear the prayer of my heart
not the words of foolish boasting.
Hear the doubts within my soul,
dark denials freezing action,
and shine your resurrection light
revealing new life.

Risen Christ,
hear the prayer of my heart
not the fear I hide behind.
Hear the longing for a fairer world,
for God's justice and compassion,
and bring your resurrection power
enabling new life.

Chris Polhill

EASTER STORY

Words and music: Pat Bennett

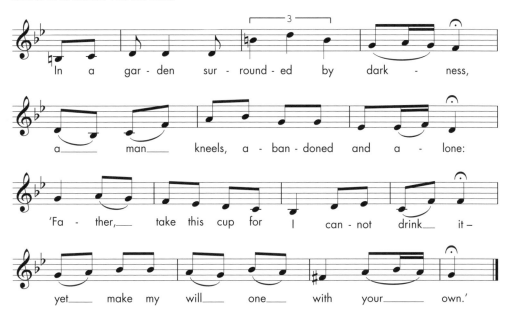

On a cross
surrounded by violence
a man hangs broken and abused:
'Father, forgive them, they don't know what they're doing.
It is finished – take my spirit back to you.'

In a tomb
surrounded by silence
a man rests waiting and contained:
'Even if you should destroy this temple –
in three days I will raise it again.'

In a garden
surrounded by sunlight
a man stands vibrantly alive:
'Go and tell my friends that I have risen
and God's Kingdom of hope has arrived.'

*Note: This is not really a congregational piece. Ideally it should be sung by two voices –
one taking the narrative part and the other the words of Jesus. However it also works all
right as a solo piece.*

*The tune is based on a variation of the Swedish folk tune 'Kvällen Stundar', which was
learnt by ear from a Swedish volunteer on Iona.*

*It should not be taken too quickly, or sung in too strict a time – the feel is very relaxed.
Sing it intuitively!*

It is perhaps best used as part of an Easter vigil service, as Easter Day dawns.

MIRACLE IN O'MEARA STREET

O'Meara Street.
A narrow London lane, a cut-through
from Union Street to Southwark Street,
with run-down office blocks,
a small factory and a warehouse.
Rubbish and fag-end strewn,
a dirty street like so many other dirty streets,
this one is further scarred
by the ugly ironwork of the railway viaduct
constantly carrying rumbling trains
full of grumbling commuters
between London Bridge and Waterloo East.

O'Meara Street.
An unfashionable street in unfashionable Southwark.
Utterly forgettable – apart from one little bit of glory.

In O'Meara Street,
right next to the railway,
so close that the trains rumble past its rooftop,
stands 'Precious Blood Catholic Church',
home of the Salvatorian Fathers.
An unremarkable brick-built edifice,
it is Victorian like its neighbours.
But, in front of the church,
beside the pavement,
in their front yard,

in a space no bigger than your kitchen,
the Salvatorian Fathers, and God, have worked a miracle:

They have created a garden!
In pots and planters grow pansies and petunias,
lilies and wallflowers and many more – more than I can name.
A riot of colour: red and gold, yellow, pink, white ...
There is even a water feature!
And all this is watched over by a smiling stone Madonna.
Smiling, no doubt, to see such beauty in an unlikely setting.

A garden in Eden expressed the Creator's hope for humankind.

A garden outside Jerusalem witnessed the renewal of that hope
as the Risen Christ said, 'Mary.'

A garden in O'Meara Street demonstrates that hope, daily,
to all who pass by.

David Lemmon

HERE IN THE HEART OF GOD

Words and music: da Noust

Here in the heart of God,_____ here in the heart of love,_____ *oh_____* wel-com-ing all our weak - ness, *oh* the Spi-rit of new life._____ *oh_____* life._____

SHOW AND TELL

If we showed you
our hands,
would you find them nicked
from building houses
for the homeless,
or calloused from using the TV remote control
too much?

If we showed you
our feet,
would you find them toughened
by walking the corridors
of a hospice
with the terminally ill,
or wrinkled
by too many hours
in the hot tub?

If we showed you
our hearts,
would you find them broken
over the struggles of
the lost, the little, the last, the least;
or would they be clogged
with the plaque
of our consumerised lives?

God of the empty grave,
show us how
to be your witnesses.

Thom M. Shuman

EASTER '78

Easter this year
seems to have slipped past
whilst I worked – on Palm Sunday,
Good Friday and Easter Day.

But it was there:
in daffodils and kid's faces
in struggle, tears and laughter
in bonfires and light in a black field,
beyond us in the stars.

It was there too
as I knelt with empty hands
to receive bread and wine,
your sharing of yourself with us.
And in words of hope –
the strength to keep going.

You are risen –
our failures lie left behind
in Friday's darkness –
and the light is shining.

Ruth Burgess

REFLECTIONS AT EASTER

'Trembling and bewildered
as they left the tomb,
speechless, saying nothing,
because they were afraid.'

Yet, one by one, and strengthened as a group,
they did believe,
and that meant telling,
'I have seen the Lord!'
Mary Magdalene, Peter, John,
Cleopas and Thomas, called the Twin.
The story without end
was now beginning.

When the stone moved,
did that reverberate
to shake the strata of fear
residing in the deserts and the Northern hills?
I wondered that, looking at the shadowy folds
of a bare Alpine hillside just before the spring.
Resurrection coming to the whole of creation
if the story's true.

No terrifying ghost to startle,
unchained from fearsome underworld;
rather, familiar Lord of fish and bread.
His 'Peace be with you',
the showing of his hands and feet,
enough to know he'd passed through death;
Lord of life, life-giving Lord in every breath.

Risen in the garden.
In the country churchyard,
daffodils about the graves,
church door open, organ playing,
waiting for the worshippers –
'No longer can thy terrors, death, appal us.' –
and I believed. Alleluia.

He took me by surprise,
although I hardly recognised
whose was that strong presence:
It happened once along the New Cross Road,
walking towards the dreaded school,
no change of my direction then,
but just a going on.

And, once again, much later,
behind me on the stairs,
none other than the Christ of Galilee.
'You can apologise,' and yes I could and did.
Quite mundane, the risen Christ,
but more real than sight or sound or touch can be,
and always there for us in bread and wine and prayer.

Liz Gregory-Smith

MISS PRINCE

For Miss Prince, daffodils meant Easter and the Resurrection of the Lord.
She told me so each Sunday around that time,
as I dutifully walked beside her, back from church.
'A miracle,' she said.
Not much joy or resurrection here, I thought.
Poor Miss Prince,
her black skirt and jacket exuded dullness, as did her tired Surrey drawl.
Elderly myself now, and a bit more able to imagine
the cold restrictions of Miss Prince's early life,
I think of her differently.
Amazing that I still remember old Miss Prince.
She did see beauty, Easter by Easter, in daffodils,
and so do I.
She took the Lord's resurrection as plain fact.
Plain fact that sustained her,
kept her a member of the small church choir,
year after year.
She wanted me, rebellious child at best,
to know that.
And I do.

Liz Gregory-Smith

THE MORIBUND CHURCH

Can these dry bones live?
Everything is possible.

Do they want vitality?
Decline need not be the end.

Do they want to come alive?
Life is risky, challenging.

Can they embrace change?
Without it they will not live.

This is Christ's *gracious* offer:

not
    continuation
        but transformation

not
    resuscitation
        but resurrection.

Judith Jessop

IT'S NOT EVEN NEWS

Hey – you up there. Just about over, is it? I wish you wouldn't drip blood like that – it really bothers me. Where did all the people go? Left you alone, have they? Crazy week, it's been. All that triumphal entry stuff, swooning crowds, poor old Pilate nearly losing his nerve this morning. Where are all those disciple characters, then? Lying low? They'd better stay out of the bars if Barabbas and his men are on the loose. And you know what? I bet the Roman scribes will never mention a thing about it. Just another crucifixion; just another dissident who got too many people worked up and had to be taken out of circulation before things got out of hand. It'll all blow over in two or three days and won't even make it into the news. They'll forget all about you and find another hopeful king of the Jews to deal with. Business as usual. Here come the women to clean you up. I'm out of here.

Oh. It's you again. You're starting to haunt me. I'll believe it when I see you in the history books, I tell you. It was all right until Saul got religion and people started getting worked up again. It was just stories to comfort your friends and discomfort the rest. Then you stirred things up all over again, and you weren't even there. Two thousand years not enough for you? Now leave me alone.

Is that you *again*? Shining through the east window? Gazing at me from an old stone slab? Singing to me from the rafters? Whispering to me from the millstream? Shouting to me from the waves breaking on the shore? Caressing me in the air blown over the wet grass? Laughing to me in the voices of children? Blowing me over in the wind on the hills? Calling to me from the streets of the city? Screaming to me from the headlines? Looking at me from the faces of the homeless? Pleading with me to listen, to listen, to listen … You never give up, do you?

O my God
I couldn't believe in you
I wanted proof
I wanted to read it in the history books
I wanted certainty
You wanted faith.

When I ran away and hid
You were there waiting for me
You came back
You never left me alone.

Andrew Foster

THE SPRING CYCLE

The Easter wheel turns –
    from the confusion of pain and bewilderment
    to the discovery of newness, life and hope.

God moves in between.

The Pentecost wheel turns –
    from the stability of life and hope
    to the confusion of mystery and challenge.

Judith Jessop

A BLESSING

The power of the Creator who brings life out of death,
be in this place.
The risen Christ be your constant companion.
The healing embrace of the Holy Spirit encircle you
so that you see resurrection ever about you.

Chris Polhill

RESURRECTION APPEARANCES

RESURRECTION

White cloth draped.
Carelessly discarded.
The cross abandoned.
Christ elsewhere.

Empty tomb.
Linen cloths crumpled.
Left behind, the trappings of death.

He moves in gardens, on dusty roads
and picnics on pebbly shores;
sits at table with us.

And yet ... eyes and spirits blind,
we haunt familiar places.
Lost pilgrims, we sanctify shells,
make shrines of empty tombs
and pray for his return,
angels' messages blocked by our litanies of death.

He is risen!

He lives.

And ever patient, smiling at our foibles,
he waits,
till, eyes and hearts open, the light dawns,
and, like Peter, we run,
shedding the cloak of old illusions,
into his warm and welcoming embrace.

Mary Hanrahan

WHAT A MORNING!

What a morning!
We were up early
after the Sabbath rest,
to do the job that women have always done,
in life as in death,
caring for bodies.

There was quite a group of us –
we'd had to watch the crucifixion at a distance,
but now that we could come close to Jesus again
we wanted to do so
as soon as we could.
So, taking with us spices and perfume
that we'd prepared,
we went to the tomb.

When we got there
the stone at the tomb's entrance
had been rolled back.
We thought perhaps there'd been another burial.
But when we went in to find the body of Jesus
it wasn't there!
We didn't know what to think
or what to do next;
and then two men came,
two men in bright cloths,
and spoke to us:
'Why are you looking among the dead for someone who is alive?'

Alive?
But we'd seen his body
taken down from the cross
and laid in this tomb.

It was incredible, unbelievable!
And then they reminded us of Jesus's words –
how he'd talked about what would happen to him,
how he'd said that he would rise to life.

When we talked to each other
we did remember him saying that.
Could it be possible?

There didn't seem a lot of point
in staying in the graveyard,
so we went and told the apostles what had happened.
They said we were talking nonsense.
Well, we knew that.
They said they didn't believe us.
Well, who would?
And as for us quoting the words of Jesus to them ...
Well, women interpreting the scriptures – whatever next!

At least Peter tried to keep an open mind,
and went to the tomb to have a look for himself.
He was as amazed as we were.

Is Jesus alive?
Is it possible?
And if he's not in the tomb, where is he?

What a morning it's been!

Ruth Burgess

EASTER HAIKUS

Through the silent air,
a calling in Galilee:
'Come, come home to God.'

Magdalene, mourning,
hears words spoken lovingly:
'Oh, weep not for me.'

With practical doubt,
Thomas, of generous heart,
sees his God revealed.

Passing the closed doors
of our hearts, comes a presence
that will not now fade.

Through the silent air,
a calling in Galilee:
'Come, come home to God.'

Margaret Moakes

RESURRECTION ENCOUNTERS

Mary Magdalene

All was tears,
even the grass
wept with dew.

Swift rain
fell,

not the racked
agony of yesterday

but gentle
sorrow
falling from between
closed eyelashes.

All was tears,
soaking every sense
and sound,

falling damp
to earth
where life
seemed buried.

All was tears;
but when at last
in soft surprise
the eyes were lifted,

they opened
onto paradise;
washed
restored

made clear
by weeping.

The upper room

Joy intruded,
disregarded locks and bolts,
trespassed on the solemn circle.

Joy interrupted,
waving fear aside
to bring fresh challenge
of fire and flame.

Joy burst in
with no apology.
It did not shuffle,
stand aside with
downcast eyes,
or wait for
a convenient break
in conversation.

Joy gatecrashed,
too eager for
the celebration
to stand on ceremony.

There never was, there never will be,
a more disruptive intruder than the bringer of Good News.

Driftwood

Gathered in the daylight
of an early morning beach,
the salt-bleached driftwood
sparked.

And looking up into the face
illuminated by the eager leap of flame,
warmth of sudden recognition
swelled inside.

All hope that had been swept away,
washed up and left to parch amongst the deadwood,
now rekindled in the heat and light
of new day's dawning.

Thomas

I long to stand once more upon
the solid ground of fact.
I am out of my depths,
and crave normality far more than hope.
Death is visceral – blood and bone;
I saw you broken,
can't withstand a second death.
Faith becomes as frail as rumour,
disillusionment the only refuge.
Do not offer me, a drowning man,
a straw of hope.
Give me your hand, beaten and bruised,
and I will clutch it.

Simon Peter

What else to do but fish?
To put out once again into the deep.

Attempting to relive the moment we first met
when life became abundant with potential.

Busyness is all. It takes away the ache of scenes
replayed each night in restless sleep.

We work, caught up in our own thoughts,
but sullen swell of sea still drags me down.

I cannot walk on water, fish for men;
however hard I trawl, I harvest nothing.

Morning sends uncertain light; instinctively
I wait to hear the crow of dawn announcing failure.

But this day brings the quiet rush of pebbles on the shore,
caught up in patterns more immense than they.

And suddenly it starts again, the second chance, replayed from the beginning –
all life around me teems with possibilities once more.

The sun breaks through the mist; I hurl myself into the sea
not caring if I sink or swim – to reach you is my only aim.

You stand there, on the edge of life, calling out against the empty fears of night;
I run to you, we sit around the flames, we eat and talk.

Three times you ask, and three times I respond;
there is new strength in each reply.

I feel you woven through my life,
know that even on strange shores you will be there.

I gather nets into my hands, they will not break.
Tomorrow I will fish again.

Lisa Debney

ENCOUNTER

Hidden Christ
reveal yourself to me.

Tear through the prejudices
which
like a veil
wrap me round
and blind and deafen me
to your presence.

Shatter the arrogant assumptions
which define where and when
I might expect
to meet you.

Throw down the image
I have made of you
which is
in reality
my own image.

Then
when I am naked
and vulnerable
stripped of everything
but openness
send me out
to encounter you afresh
in the resurrection garden
of your world.

Pat Bennett

PETER AND MARY

John 20:17–18; Luke 24:10–11

A: Peter –

B: Mmmm hm? *(Does not turn round)*

A: Peter –

B: Yes.

A: Peter –

B: A drink? Oh, thanks – put it down here ...

A: Peter, I need to talk to you.

B: Not now: I'm extremely busy.

A: This is important.

B: Look here, madam. I don't know who you are. Maybe one of the delegates from the Mothers and Toddlers group who pestered us until we managed to make an appointment with Jesus ...

A: That's not quite how I remember it ...

B: But you must be reasonable. We are very busy men. You seem to think the Kingdom of Heaven is like a little child – drop everything when it needs you. But there's a lot of paperwork.

A: I'm sorry.

B: You don't need to be sorry. I've been given this responsibility. By Jesus himself – 'On this rock' – it's a privilege. But I'm afraid administration means less time for pastoral care. We have to delegate. Anyway, I don't know why I'm using valuable time telling you all this. Don't worry your pretty little head about it.

A: But I have a message for you.

B: Why didn't you say so in the first place? Women – they take so long to come to the point. And they're so emotional ... well?

A: It's about Jesus.

B: My good woman, let's get this straight. We, the disciples, are the ones to tell the world about Jesus. That's our job. Your job is to listen.

A: But I am one of the disciples.

B: Huh?

A: One of your fellow disciples – if you can count beyond twelve: all the others who followed Jesus, and talked with him, and shared the good news they heard with the others.

B: Ah, well, of course I'm very much in favour of lay ministry.

A: Discipleship.

B: But, dear lady, I am surprised that you can call yourself a 'fellow' disciple. Rather a male term for such liberated times. However, I don't want to disparage the wonderful work done by those behind the scenes. The ministry of Jesus, and our own now, wouldn't have been possible without those who prepared the meals, washed up, offered hospitality ... The ladies, God bless them, where would we be without them!

A: We learned a lot from Jesus about serving.

B: Oh yes, washing feet – a very moving symbolic gesture. I'm thinking of making it a yearly ritual.

A: ... About Jesus ...

B: Ah, you felt you had something to say. Well, get it off your chest, my child. We're here to listen.

A: Jesus is alive.

B: Don't be ridiculous!

A: Jesus is alive.

B: Are you trying to tell me?

A: Jesus is alive.

B: Ah, well, metaphorically, yes – 'He lives within my heart.' But you know, at this difficult time we have to come to terms with grief.

A: I saw him.

B: You saw him. Look, madam, I am Peter, and I didn't see him. Who do you think you are?

A: I'm Mary.

B: Oh yes, one of the faithful Marys!

A: Sister of Martha.

B: Now ... Martha ... I remember – she was in charge of the catering committee. A formidable woman.

A: She is also a very perceptive woman. When our brother Lazarus died, she talked to Jesus about resurrection and faith. She said, 'Lord, I now believe that you are the Messiah, the Son of God, who was to come into the world.'

B: No – that was me at Caesarea Philippi. I said, 'You are the Messiah.' How can a mere woman be expected to grasp such a profound truth? We must set the record straight.

A: But I want to tell you what is happening right now – Jesus is alive. I went to the tomb. It was empty. I thought they had taken Jesus away. I came and told you.

B: Yes, yes. I know. I saw the empty tomb.

A: And?

B: And I realised that it represented a deep theological truth which needs to be interpreted to the laity through exposition and liturgy. Centuries of scholarship will emerge from that empty tomb.

A: But that's not all.

B: My dear – that's quite enough to be going on with.

A: Peter.

B: Don't touch me.

A: That's what he said.

B: Huh?

A: Jesus.

B: During his lifetime he did have an alarmingly permissive attitude to the fairer sex. He did let them touch him, and talk to him, and share meals with him. People began to talk. I think we can move toward a less threatening situation in the Church, with women playing their part but knowing their place.

A: I'm talking about now. Everything has changed – that's why I wasn't to cling to the past. I have just seen the Lord. He is alive. He gave me this message: 'Go to my brothers and tell them that I am now ascending to my Father and your Father, my God and your God.'

B: My God *(turns round).*

A: And mine.

A & B: Our God. Who do we tell now?

Jan Sutch Pickard

EMMAUS WAY

(Tune: Gonaflon Royal)

Along the road that leads to faith,
life's varied rhythms all must meet;
through light and darkness, life and death,
before our journey is complete.

Along the road Christ makes a space
to walk with those in burdened gloom
of pain's self-loathing and disgrace,
to love them well, and give them room.

'Your presence turns our thoughts about
and shifts our feet from blank retreat.
You light the candles death blows out;
your new reality we meet.'

'Come in and rest and share our meal;
the way is long, the day near done.'
The broken bread unveils the real:
before us stands the risen One.

When faith is hard and long the night,
when grey despair on our path lies,
open our eyes to your new light:
show us God's Easter, Love's surprise.

Leith Fisher

TWO FRIENDS

Luke 24:13–33

A/B: Two friends
          on our way
A: on the dusty road:
B: talking, listening,
A: sharing pain and confusion.

A: Another
      walks with us –
B: unknown –
A: looks into our eyes,
B: listens to lost hopes
      and wild rumours.

A: He speaks; we hear
      the story of salvation
      as though for the first time,
A/B: as we travel on.

A: We have arrived;
B: he wants to go further –
      on his way;
A: we ask him to stay,
      as dusk falls
      on the dusty road.
B: We go indoors,
      sit, tired, at a table
      to share a meal.
A: He takes bread, blesses it,
      breaks and offers it to us
B: who then see who is our companion –
A: but he has gone.

A/B: We remember
B: the journey, the words we heard,
A: the everyday presence of road, table,
      and broken bread –
B: we know the news that must be shared.

A: We cannot stay put,
B: but, here and now, set out,
      back along the dusty road:
A/B: two friends
      on God's way.

Jan Sutch Pickard

AN EMMAUS ROAD LITURGY OF COMMITMENT FROM IONA ABBEY

Preparation: Place three bowls containing different-coloured pieces of wool in the centre of the worship space: a bowl of green wool, a bowl of red wool, a bowl of blue wool.

Opening responses

Song: O where are you going? (John L. Bell and Graham Maule, *Heaven Shall Not Wait*, Wild Goose Publications)

Reading: Luke 24:13–35 (*read dramatically if possible*)

Reflection and invitation to commitment

These two disciples were coming away from the intensity of the past few days in Jerusalem. They had lived through the last week of Jesus's life and now felt that the way they had been following – Jesus's way – had come to a dead end. They couldn't make sense of it. It seemed so pointless. They needed to get away, to go home presumably: to go back to how life had been before Jesus.

But then they found (as they later came to understand it) that Jesus – the risen Jesus – had joined them on their journey.

I want to pick out three things from this story, and to link those things to the invitation to commitment I want to make to you.

First, this story wouldn't *be* a story if these two disciples hadn't welcomed the stranger into their conversation, and then later into their home. So, there is first a challenge to show hospitality to the stranger. For, 'As the lark says in her song: *Often, often, often goes Christ is the stranger's guise'*.

Secondly, it is a very *real* story, in that the stranger helps them to make sense of something in their lives. How many of you, in talking with a stranger – on a train or at a youth hostel or wherever – have been enabled to understand something in your own life better? I have. I have been helped to make sense of, and to withstand, an experience of suffering through talking with a stranger.

And then, thirdly – after Christ has vanished from their sight – they go tell their fellow disciples about their encounter with the risen Lord.

After the next song, you are invited to come forward to the crossing and to take a piece of wool:

Green – if you want to commit yourself to welcoming a stranger.

Red – if you want to commit yourself to sharing with someone how you have come to make sense of an experience of suffering.

Blue – if you want to commit yourself to sharing with a fellow believer your experience or understanding of the risen Christ.

Song: The love of God comes close (John L. Bell and Graham Maule, *Enemy and Apathy*, Wild Goose Publications)

Sign of commitment: Taking the strands of wool ...

Prayer of dedication

Risen Lord Jesus, be present with us now.
Help us to be open to you in the stranger's guise.
Come alongside us, and help us to find new purpose in the painful and wasted
     experiences of our lives.
And give us friends and fellow disciples with whom we may share our experience
     of your risen presence.
Amen

Affirmation of faith

Song

Closing responses

Blessing

Richard Sharples

Note: Responses and an affirmation of faith for this service can be found in Iona Abbey Worship Book, *Wild Goose Publications*

PRAYERS ON THE EMMAUS ROAD

Ezekiel 37:1–14, The valley of dry bones; Luke 24:13–35, The journey to Emmaus

Out of Ezekiel's prophecy and vision in times of extremity, we pray:

Eternal God,
whose promise is the gift of life
to those who remain faithful to your Word,
renew the breath of your Spirit within us
that we may find your presence in our hearts
and your courage in our lives.
Re-member us and bring us to the place of your intention,
where dry land becomes fertile,
dead water flows clean again
and a bleak future comes alive with hope
in the Risen Christ.

Chant: Goodness is stronger than evil (Words: Bishop Desmond Tutu; music: John L. Bell, *There is One Among Us*, Wild Goose Publications)

On the road to Emmaus, two followers of Jesus were talking about what had happened to him. They did not yet know that he was risen. They were in darkness and could not yet pray as we can pray in our dark times:

Dying Jesus,
whose final human pain
was a sense of abandonment by God,
look mercifully on this suffering humanity
that we who endure the evil of this world
may enter into your transformation of it,
and in so doing come again into hearing range
of our heavenly Father, whose love is stronger than death
and to whom we pray in your name.

Chant: Goodness is stronger than evil

As the two followers talked, Jesus drew near, but they did not see that he was the Risen Christ. When we do not recognise how close Jesus is to us, we may pray:

Saving God,
to whom the darkness and the light are both alike,

enter into the dark places of our lives
and fill them with what you want us to see.
Take our blindness and give us new vision for the way ahead;
take our fear and give us fresh courage for the path
that leads to the fulfilment of our lives:
for the sake of your beloved human race
made perfect in your beloved Son, Jesus.

Chant: Goodness is stronger than evil

In answer to Jesus's questions, the followers told their story, his story, and he opened
the scriptures to them. We pray for our eyes to be opened to God's Word.

All-seeing and unseen God,
you make your presence known to us when we least expect it.
Come to us, we pray, when our need is greatest;
and when we have forgotten need and least think of you.
Give us peace when we are troubled;
disturb us when we are complacent.
When we are locked into darkness, release us.
When we are neglectful of the darkness, open our eyes
to see the one who overcame the powers of darkness for our sakes.

Chant: Goodness is stronger than evil

As they neared the end of their journey, the two followers invited Jesus to supper. Only
then did they realise who he was. We pray to be aware of Jesus in the world today.

God of darkness and light,
we see you not as you are but as we are.
Take these clouded lenses from our eyes.
Unprotected from your brightness,
make us not so dazzled by your purity,
or so blinded by your perfection,
or so horror-struck by your integrity
that we fail to see you all around us
in the struggle of our lives.
Through the holiness of your Spirit.

Chant: Goodness is stronger than evil

At the end of the journey, the two followers knew resurrection joy. With great energy, they walked the seven miles back to Jerusalem to tell the other disciples. We too give thanks for the Saviour's presence in our daily lives.

Living Jesus,
whose presence on our daily road
we fail to see in the grief that surrounds us,
warm our hearts with fresh confidence in your Word
so that, in making room for the stranger beside us,
we find your hospitality awaiting us,
and the reassurance of your presence
to inspire us to tread the road again
and share the good news of your resurrection life.

Chant: Goodness is stronger than evil

These prayers may be closed by the words of the Grace or by another suitable prayer.

Terry Garley

EMMAUS ROAD

We are disappointed and worn down.
Lord, walk with us.

We doubt what we believe.
Lord, teach us.

We need a sign.
Lord, break the bread.

We seek your kingdom.
Lord, fill our hearts with fire.

Nick Burden

EMMAUS NOW

Words: Leith Fisher
Music: Timothy Redman   Arrangement: Sandy Small

rest, sit down and with us stay.

Come now, come share our bread.

3. In his hands the com-mon bread he takes. Then the loaf fa -

mi - liar lifts and breaks.   Dark - en'd minds ex-

-plode with new - found light:

Friend and Lord is   here and dear to   sight.

4. Stran-ger no more   come to our ta - ble spread.

Meet_ us as Lord and   our all - glo-rious Head.   Con-

- firm in   us that death   it - self lies   dead   through

blood and life_____ out - poured_____ now won - - - drous - ly re - stored.

I KNOW THAT MY REDEEMER LIVETH

I met him in the garden –
for when he called my name
I knew,
deep within my soul,
this was my love,
my hope,
my very life
come back to me again.
'Mary,' he said,
so gentle then,
so real,
so intimate with me.
And then I knew
all would be well.
'I know that my Redeemer liveth.'
For who could call my name
like this,
and thus redeem me from
my brokenness
and give me life again
when Life had died.

I met him in an upper room –
for when he looked into my eyes
I knew,
deep in my mind,
this was my chance,
my opening,
my opportunity
now to believe.
'Thomas,' he said,
forgiving me my unbelief –
so great,
so marvellous this acceptance.
And then I knew
I could believe.
'I know that my Redeemer liveth.'
For who could look me in the eye
like this,

and thus redeem me from
my unbelief,
and give me purpose now
when Faith had died.

I met him by the lakeside –
for when he challenged me
I knew,
deep in my being,
this was my task,
my call,
my true discipleship
so clear and real again.
'Peter,' he said –
so right,
so challenging for me.
And then I understood
what I must do.
'I know that my Redeemer liveth.'
For who could know my sins
like this
and thus redeem me from
denial's pain,
and give me sheep and lambs to feed
when Love had died.

I met him in my wanderings –
for when he chose my life
I knew,
deep in my heart,
this was my time,
my birth,
my new beginning,
obedience to his Way.
'My child,' he said,
so risen then,
so true,
so real for me.
And then I saw once more
the way to go.
'I know that my Redeemer liveth.'

For who'd believe in me
like this,
and thus redeem me from
my past,
and give me God again
when He had died.

Tom Gordon

THOMAS'S STORY

It was different for me;
maybe it had to be.

All of my life it had been the same,
the same as my twin brother –
the same clothes,
the same first day at school – at the synagogue,
the same birthday – often the same presents.
Even the same name, if people got us mixed up.

Jesus was the first person
who really treated me as an individual.
He knew what was important to me.
He knew what made me, me.

So maybe, on reflection, Jesus had his reasons
to meet with the other disciples
when I wasn't there.

It was a strange week for me.
Everyone was talking about angels and ghosts,
about stolen bodies,
about journeys and broken bread.

I didn't know what to believe.
I needed to see Jesus for myself –
and a week later I did.

He stood in front of me
naming me – Thomas –
inviting me to touch him

to make sure for myself
that he was flesh and blood.

It was different for me –
but maybe it's different for everyone.

Jesus names each one of us,
and invites us into his risen life.

Ruth Burgess

SCARS REVEAL RESURRECTION

(from a sermon)

John 20:19–31; Acts 4:32–35

Jesus shows them his hands and his side, shows the hideous piercing that nails and spear have inflicted; and the second time he comes to the upper room he not only shows his wounds and scars but invites Thomas to touch them. The very fact that Jesus has to do this tells us that just seeing Jesus wasn't enough: it was too shocking, too mind-blowing, too confusing to see Jesus standing there clearly alive – when they knew he had died by crucifixion. It is the reality of the scars and wounds that Jesus bears that reveals to the disciples the extraordinary truth of the Resurrection.

It is easy for Easter to be a joyful time after the discipline of Lent. A bright celebration of spring and new life after (in our hemisphere of the world) the cold, grey winter. But resurrection is so much more than that. True, it is joyful, but not a kind of bubbly party joy; true it is about new life, but it's about so much more than the life bursting out of the ground all around us. Resurrection is seen in the places of damage – in the scars and wounds of life where we allow God to Easter within us. Because resurrection is about the very different pattern that God puts onto the harsh things of life that we bring to him. Resurrection never denies the pain and wounds of life: it is not a pretty picture covering up nasty things. It is the reality of God with us; it is the difference God makes; it is the confusing change that turns our ideas upside down – but gives us life and hope again.

We are Easter people – Christianity would have withered away without Easter; a longing to see and recognise resurrection should be at the heart of our prayers for ourselves, the world and the Church. But we doubt like Thomas; we doubt the reality of Jesus's resurrection, and most particularly we doubt that the Resurrection is for our life today. We, like countless Christians before us, push resurrection and all it means away until we die, and talk or sing of this life – this amazing gift of life – as hard, as a vale of tears, as only struggle and suffering, as though somehow this life we live is perpetually in Good Friday and never reaches Easter. But it is just there, in all those hard and painful places, that we should pray for and expect resurrection. We forget that when Martha confronts Jesus with his failure to turn up and heal Lazarus, Jesus tells her that to know him is to be part of his resurrection life in the here and now.

Maybe resurrection is too uncomfortable, too confusing, and we would rather leave it till we face death. Having our ideas, our expectations, our whole way of life turned upside down is uncomfortable – change is disturbing. Perhaps that is why the wounded and the desperate are more willing to consider it. Change then can only be for the better.

Just stop and think, in these great days of Easter, where you would like to see resurrection: God's pattern on the wounds and scars of life that daunt you. Perhaps where you personally struggle with illness, disappointment, relationship issues – what would resurrection mean for you there, what needs to change? Or in the Church, where we struggle to communicate the gospel to our culture today. Or in the world – where there is so much violence. I long to see resurrection in Iraq, in Palestine/Israel, in the places where children are hungry, uneducated, without health care. And I only have to start naming these wounded and scarred places to underline that resurrection is no soft option, does not come with the wave of a wand, and will need our willingness for God to Easter within us. Easter people need to be tough, to be willing to stay with the Cross, with struggle and pain for resurrection to come. We would know nothing of the resurrection of Jesus if his followers had not radically changed their lives – and risked their lives – to be sure that the message and the life his resurrection gave was not lost. They lived with Easter within them, and gave their energies to aid the resurrection energies of God; it's a good model. I know of people who have come to faith because everywhere they went to help in our society – in prison, with Amnesty International, with Refugee Aid – they found Christians there, working in the hard, painful places for resurrection to come.

Resurrection is at the heart of our faith; it is for every aspect of our lives today; it is worth our energy and our prayer; it is worth the challenge to our comfort, and the pain and wounds from staying with the hard and the difficult. Look for it, work for it, and may God Easter in you.

Chris Polhill

*'Easter in us' comes from the Gerard Manley Hopkins poem 'The Wreck of the Deutschland'.

ACTS OF THE APOSTLES

Peter: Transformation
John 21

Peter
hothead
reacting
overreacting
never truly listening

But

always passionate
not one to shrink

Until

that awful day
those denials
that cock crow
piercing
your soul

His remembered gaze
drawing your tears
how crushed you were

Then
when he returned
did you imagine
he would 'have a word'
for you?

Fearing his rejection?
Startled by his command?
'Feed my sheep.'
Said three times

Cancelling out
your denials
Freeing you to become
the rock of the Church, his Body
Releasing your passion
for his Word, his people

Where would we be without you, Peter?

Thomas: My twin
John 20:24–29

Ah Thomas, as a doubter, I am glad
that you were present
when the Lord revealed himself
in those days of hurt and pain.

Like me you knew the need
for the earthly sense of presence.
It is not that faith is absent
but we still need our Lord embodied.

Stephen: Holy ground
Acts 6, 7

Stephen, you were beautiful
with passion for the Lord,
Truth shining from you
as you preached the holy Word.

People were astounded,
offended by your zeal,
pierced by your honesty,
knowing you were real.

And they could not bear reality,
confronted by their sin,
so they plotted and protested,
resolved to do you in.

They stoned you, brutalised you,
refused what they had heard;
as you gave up your spirit
you cried out to the Lord.

What they could not do in life
they have not achieved in death,
for like Christ's your story shimmers
with the radiance of new birth.

And when we are persecuted,
brought low by evil all around,
we still have visions of your beauty
to keep our feet on holy ground.

On the road
Acts 8:26–39

Perhaps people do not travel
in chariots today,
but the roads
still have travellers
who are looking for their God.

Resident aliens
Acts 7:6–7

Through history we discover
how little we have learned.

We still enslave, mistreat,
refuse sanctuary,
don't befriend.

'But I will judge the nation that they serve,' said God.
He will find us wanting,
lacking the justice of our God

Times of refreshing
Acts 3:19–21

OH HOW I LONG FOR THOSE TIMES OF REFRESHING
THAT COME FROM THE PRESENCE OF THE LORD

When doubts and demons assail me,
in the dead of night and at noon,
telling me the promise is broken,
that this world has only its wounds.

OH HOW I LONG FOR THOSE TIMES OF REFRESHING
THAT COME FROM THE PRESENCE OF THE LORD

When I cannot make sense of the Word,
when I feel a hostage to fate,
when I cannot be real with my God,
fearing judgement and knowledge too great.

OH HOW I LONG FOR THOSE TIMES OF REFRESHING
THAT COME FROM THE PRESENCE OF THE LORD

When I fail to be one in community –
caught up in my own woes and pain,
ignoring the value of others
whose presence is all for my gain.

OH HOW I LONG FOR THOSE TIMES OF REFRESHING
THAT COME FROM THE PRESENCE OF THE LORD.

I can give you my heart once again,
though poor and unworthy it seems,
for I know if I hold to my visions
you promise me more than false dreams.

OH HOW I LONG FOR THOSE TIMES OF REFRESHING
THAT COME FROM THE PRESENCE OF THE LORD

Yvonne Morland

THE PICNIC

(Tune: Teddy Bears' Picnic)

1. One day some fishermen took their boat
    and went out on the sea.
    Their names were Peter and James and John
    and Andrew from Galilee.
    They fished all night, but all in vain;
    a voice from the shore called, 'Try again' –
    and then they found they'd lots of fish for breakfast.

2. When they got back to the shore they found
   that Jesus was waiting there;
   he'd made a picnic of fish and bread
   for him and his friends to share.
   They shared the food till all were fed;
   he was their Lord, risen from the dead,
   and they were glad to be with him for breakfast.

Margaret Harvey

AT THE LAKESIDE

It was the lad, John, who saw him first;
we were too busy hanging onto the bulging net,
and maybe just a bit resentful of a stranger on the shore
telling us our business.
'It's him,' he said.
'Who?' I asked, as I straightened up.
'It's the Lord – who else?' he replied
with a grin too wide for his face.

I shaded my eyes against the low dawn light and stared,
and my heart leapt – and froze – within my chest.
I grabbed up my garments and plunged over the side of the boat,
sinking to waist level in the waves, as I had before
when he'd called me to come to him across the water.
Struggling up the shingle, I fell in a heap at his feet,
and he grabbed my hands, as he had that other time,
and hauled me up till we were eye to eye.
The others arrived, bustling up the beach, bringing fish
to lay on the fire beside the little loaves already baking there.
'Come and eat,' he said, as he broke the bread and shared the feast.

Afterwards, when everyone was sated and settled,
he looked at me across the fire.
'Walk with me,' he said,
and we set off along the shoreline.
'Simon, do you love me more than these?' he asked,
indicating the others sprawled out on the sand.
'Yes, Lord,' I answered automatically. 'You know I love you.'

'Feed my flock,' he said.
A little further on he asked again: 'Simon, do you love me?'
'Yes, Lord,' I said again. 'You know I love you.'
'Look after my lambs,' he said.

And then,
he asked me a third time:
'Simon, do you love me?'
He gazed into my tear-filled eyes
and we were back in the courtyard beside another fire.
'Lord, you know everything,' I cried. 'You know I love you.'
'Lead my sheep,' he said, and smiled,
and the sun rose in the sky, and the sea shimmered,
and the world was wonderful.

I looked back and saw the lad was following.
'What about him, Lord?' I asked.
He turned, regarding John with that look of love
reserved for children and for all pure-hearted ones.
'Not your concern,' he chided gently.
'You, you follow me.'
And I did
to the end ...

Carol Dixon

EARLY THIS MORNING

Early this morning I met a child
on her way to school.
Dragging her feet,
huddled against
March's liony wind,
she gave me a smile,
but I was too busy
looking for you
to really notice.

At noon,
as I walking home for lunch,
I met a neighbour
trailing his dog;
he nodded
and asked how I was,
but in my rush to get to the house
to see if you were waiting,
I had no time for a chat.

Tonight
my wife tiptoed
into the quiet of my den,
bringing me a cup of tea and
kissing me softly on the cheek
before slipping out,
but I was too busy
searching the Bible
to really notice.

Thom M. Shuman

EASTERTIDE PRAYERS OF INTERCESSION

Based on the Easter appearances of Jesus

Open our eyes
WE LONG TO SEE YOU

As we wonder at your resurrection,
at the hope you have given us,
we remember
the appearances you made to those close to you,
and we pray that our eyes, too,
may be opened to your presence.

Open our eyes
WE LONG TO SEE YOU

We think of Thomas,
so full of doubt.
Yet you recognised his need
to be reassured by your presence.
We offer you our concerns for our world.
Sometimes it is hard to see your presence
in events that unfold.
Comfort us and take away our doubt
as we pray for reconciliation
and hope in the world in which we live.

Open our eyes
WE LONG TO SEE YOU

We think of Peter,
the rock on which you built your Church,
so full of assurance and commitment
and then so afraid and upset to have betrayed you.
Yet you appeared
to reassure him of your love
and commanded him to feed your lambs.
We offer you the Church worldwide,
and our church here at _____.
Give us reassurance
and openness to your guiding direction.

Open our eyes
WE LONG TO SEE YOU

We think of the women who went to your tomb,
so sad and wanting to be near you,
even in their disillusionment.
You appeared to them
in the form of angels
proclaiming the good news of your resurrection;
and the women, full of joy, rushed back to tell the good news.
We offer ourselves
and ask for your reassurance to help us reach out
to the communities in which we live and work.
We pray that we will make a difference to other people's lives
by sharing all that you have given us;
that, through grace,
lives may be changed
by your presence.

Open our eyes
WE LONG TO SEE YOU

We think of Mary,
who loved you so much
and took such risks to be close to you.
We think of how you recognised her need to see you –
how you wiped away her tears
simply by speaking her name.
We name before you
those we know to be in special need at this time –
those who are sick, lonely and afraid ...
Enfold them with your love and presence.
Be close to each of them, and to others not known to us
but known to you.

Open our eyes
WE LONG TO SEE YOU

We think of Cleopas and his friend,
who walked their lonely road to Emmaus,
a journey of sadness
after all the events of Holy Week.

Yet you walked beside them
and shared with them –
opening their eyes to your presence
in the breaking of the bread at supper.
Journey alongside all those who are bereaved at this time,
especially ...

Open our eyes
WE LONG TO SEE YOU

In silence
we remember those
who journeyed with us
and have moved on
into your eternal presence
where their eyes are fully opened
to your love
and glory.

We thank you
for your presence
with us
now
and
always.

Amen

Ruth Bowen

OPENING AND CLOSING
RESPONSES FOR EASTERTIDE

EASTER DAY

Cycles A, B, C, *see p. 20*

SECOND SUNDAY OF EASTER

Cycle A

Acts 2:42–47; Ps 118; 1 Pet 1:3–9; Jn 20:19–31

In the breaking of bread and in prayers
JESUS IS AMONG US

In the telling of stories and in signs
JESUS IS AMONG US

In the sharing of resources and in justice
JESUS IS AMONG US

In this place and in this moment
JESUS IS AMONG US IN JOY

> A great mercy and a sure hope
> A new birth and a deep peace
> A strong love and a rich blessing
> GOD IS SENDING US OUT IN JOY

THIRD SUNDAY OF EASTER

Cycle A

Acts 2:14, 22–28; Ps 16; 1 Pet 1:17–21; Lk 24:13–35

You take us seriously
YOU LISTEN TO OUR QUESTIONS

You walk alongside us
YOU SHARE OUR JOURNEYS

You surprise us and bless us
YOU FILL US WITH WONDER

You call us together
YOU CALL US TO LIFE

> Open our eyes to see you amongst us
> BURN IN OUR HEARTS AND FILL US WITH JOY

> Open our minds to the truth of your story
> DANCE WITH US THE CEILIDH OF LIFE

FOURTH SUNDAY OF EASTER

Cycle A

Acts 2:14, 36–41; Ps 23; 1 Pet 1:20–25; Jn 10:1–10

The light is shining
WE ARE WELCOME HERE

The door is open
WE ARE WELCOME HERE

The meal is ready
WE ARE WELCOME HERE

The invitation is for us and our children
THIS IS THE PLACE WHERE WE BELONG

> Coming and going
> GOD WATCHES OVER US

> Resting and travelling
> GOD WATCHES OVER US

> Through good and through evil
> GOD WATCHES OVER US

> All the days of our lives
> GOD SAFEGUARDS US WITH LOVE

FIFTH SUNDAY OF EASTER

Cycle A

Acts 6:1–7; Ps 33; 1 Pet 2:4–9; Jn 14:1–12

Sharing stories, sharing food
THIS IS OUR LIFE

Sharing wisdom, sharing hope
THIS IS OUR TRUTH

Sharing laughter, sharing pain
THIS IS OUR WAY

We are living stones
WE ARE THE HOUSEHOLD OF GOD

>   We are travelling the way of justice
>   WE ARE EXPLORING THE WAY OF TRUTH
>
>   We are living the life of discoverers
>   WE ARE JOURNEYING HOME TO GOD

SIXTH SUNDAY OF EASTER

Cycle A

Acts 8:5–8,14–17; Ps 66; 1 Pet 1:15–18; Jn 14:15–21

Come and hear
THE GOOD NEWS OF GOD

Come and see
WHAT JESUS HAS DONE

We will tell the story of God in our world
WE WILL SHARE THE SECRET OF HOPE IN OUR LIVES

Come and explore the truth of the gospel
COME AND RECEIVE THE HOLY SPIRIT OF GOD

>   We are loved, cherished, befriended, accepted
>   THIS IS THE TRUTH

We are not alone: God's love is in us
THIS IS THE TRUTH

God knows our hopes, our fears, our questions
THIS IS THE TRUTH

God is leading us deep into justice and wonder
GOD IS JOYFULLY WALKING US HOME

ASCENSION DAY

Cycles A, B, C, *see page 138*

SEVENTH SUNDAY OF EASTER

Cycle A

Acts 1:12–14; Ps 27; 1 Pet 4:13–16; Jn 17:1–11

Old and young
WE SEEK YOUR FACE

Happy and sad
WE SEEK YOUR FACE

Strong and weak
WE SEEK YOUR FACE

You are our light and our help
YOU ARE THE SWEETNESS OF OUR NIGHTS AND DAYS

Named as Christians
WE ARE IN THE WORLD

Taught and trusted
WE ARE IN THE WORLD

Blessed and prayed for
WE ARE IN THE WORLD

We belong to God
WE ARE NOT ALONE

PENTECOST SUNDAY

Cycle A, B, C, *see page 148*

TRINITY SUNDAY

Cycle A, *see page 200*

SECOND SUNDAY OF EASTER

Cycle B

Acts 4:32–35; Ps 118; 1 Jn 5:1–6; Jn 20:19–31

What do Christians do?
THEY SHARE THEIR POSSESSIONS

What do Christians do?
THEY CARE FOR EACH OTHER

What do Christians do?
THEY SPEAK ABOUT JESUS

What do they do?
THEY LIVE A NEW LIFE

    In us, among us
    THE PEACE OF JESUS

    In us, among us
    THE PRESENCE OF JESUS

    In us, among us
    THE POWER OF JESUS

    In us, among us
    GOD'S LIFE AND GOD'S LOVE

THIRD SUNDAY OF EASTER

Cycle B

Acts 3:13–15, 17–19; Ps 4; 1 Jn 2:1–5; Lk 24:35–48

What can bring us happiness?
THE LOVE OF GOD AMONG US

What can bring us happiness?
THE JUSTICE OF GOD AROUND US

What can bring us happiness?
THE BREATH OF GOD WITHIN US

Open our minds to the scriptures
OPEN OUR EYES TO JESUS IN OUR MIDST

> Love of God
> GROW IN US
>
> Fire of God
> REFINE US
>
> Laughter of God
> DANCE IN US
>
> Justice of God
> DEFINE US
>
> Tears of God
> WEEP IN US
>
> Beauty of God
> CARESS US
>
> Story of God
> RUN DEEP IN US
>
> Mystery of God
> BLESS US

Or:

> We are witnesses
> TO THE LOVE OF GOD OUR MAKER

We are witnesses
TO THE PEACE THAT JESUS GIVES US

We are witnesses
TO THE HOLY SPIRIT IN OUR LIVES

Surprised, challenged, healed and nourished,
WE GO OUT IN JUSTICE AND JOY

FOURTH SUNDAY OF EASTER

Cycle B

Acts 4:8–12; Ps 118; 1 Jn 3:1–2; Jn 10:11–18

Children of God
THIS IS WHAT WE ARE

People of God
THIS IS WHO WE ARE

Give thanks to God, for God is good,
THE LOVE OF GOD IS NOW AND FOR EVER

> Holy and just
> MAKE US LIKE JESUS

> Ready to take risks
> MAKE US LIKE JESUS

> Willing to weep
> MAKE US LIKE JESUS

> Aware that we're loved
> MAKE US LIKE JESUS

> When people meet us
> MAY THEY MEET GOD IN US

> So be it, Holy Spirit
> AMEN

FIFTH SUNDAY OF EASTER

Cycle B

Acts 9:26–31; Ps 22; 1 Jn 3:18–24; Jn 15:1–8

In the midst of creation,
in the fields and the city,
to all who will listen
I WILL TELL OF YOUR LOVE

In the company of the poor,
in the presence of the mighty,
to all who will listen
I WILL TELL OF YOUR LOVE

Your love is more than words
Your love is real and active
To all who will listen
I WILL TELL OF YOUR LOVE

    Heard and valued
    Freed and forgiven
    WE GO INTO THE WORLD
    TO BEAR MUCH FRUIT

    Fed and nourished
    Loved and cherished
    WE GO INTO THE WORLD
    TO BEAR MUCH FRUIT

    Today and tomorrow
    Rooted in Jesus
    WE GO INTO THE WORLD
    TO BEAR MUCH FRUIT

SIXTH SUNDAY OF EASTER

Cycle B

Acts 10:25–26, 34–35, 44–48; Ps 98; 1 Jn 4:7–10; Jn 15:9–17

God is a God of grace and salvation
There is no way we can buy God's favour
GOD HAS NO FAVOURITES, GOD IS LOVE

Jesus shared his life with all kinds of people
Jesus told the story of the Good Samaritan
JESUS HAS NO FAVOURITES, JESUS IS LOVE

The Holy Spirit dances in the mystery of creation
The Holy Spirit delights in wisdom and in justice
THE HOLY SPIRIT HAS NO FAVOURITES, THE HOLY SPIRIT IS LOVE

    Into our streets and homes we go
    LIVING OUR LIVES IN GOD'S LOVE

    Into our joys and sorrows we go
    LIVING OUR LIVES IN GOD'S LOVE

    Into the fight for justice we go
    LIVING OUR LIVES IN GOD'S LOVE

    Blessed with the friendship of God we go
    LIVING OUR LIVES IN GOD'S LOVE

ASCENSION DAY

Cycle B, *see page 139*

SEVENTH SUNDAY OF EASTER

Cycle B

Acts 1:15–17, 20–26; Ps 103; 1 Jn 4:11–16; Jn 17:11–19

In my living and in my loving
YOU HAVE BLESSED ME

In my tears and in my laughter
YOU HAVE BLESSED ME

In my sisters and in my brothers
YOU HAVE BLESSED ME

With everything that's in me
I GIVE YOU THANKS

> Growing in us
> GOD'S LAUGHTER

> Growing in us
> GOD'S GLORY

> Growing in us
> GOD'S KINDNESS

> Growing in us
> GOD'S LOVE

TRINITY SUNDAY

Cycle B, *see page 200*

SECOND SUNDAY OF EASTER

Cycle C

Acts 5:12–16; Ps 118; Rev 1:9–13, 17–19; Jn 20:19–31

Sometimes believing, sometimes doubting
WE COME TO GOD'S HOUSE

Sometimes weeping, sometimes laughing
WE COME TO GOD'S HOUSE

Sometimes afraid, sometimes joyful
WE COME TO GOD'S HOUSE

Whatever has happened to us, here we are welcome
THIS DAY AND THIS HOUSE BELONG TO GOD

> As God sent Jesus
> JESUS SENDS US
>
> To bring hope and healing
> JESUS SENDS US
>
> To care for our neighbours
> JESUS SENDS US
>
> To work for justice
> JESUS SENDS US
>
> With the gift of the Holy Spirit
> JESUS SENDS US
> JESUS SENDS US WITH LOVE

THIRD SUNDAY OF EASTER

Cycle C

Acts 5:27–32, 40–41; Ps 30; Rev 5:11–14; Jn 21:1–19

In the night
and in the morning,
WE WILL COME TO YOU

Full of sadness,
tired and hungry,
WE WILL COME TO YOU

Lost and puzzled,
glad and hopeful,
WE WILL COME TO YOU

You welcome us and feed us
YOU QUESTION US WITH LOVE

    Take our hands in your hands
    YOU KNOW THAT WE LOVE YOU

    Wrap our lives in your life
    YOU KNOW THAT WE TRUST YOU

    Call our names in friendship
    YOU KNOW THAT WE WILL FOLLOW YOU

    Risen Jesus
    SEND US OUT IN JUSTICE AND JOY

FOURTH SUNDAY OF EASTER

Cycle C

Acts 13:14, 43–52; Ps 100; Rev 7:9, 14–17; Jn 10:27–30

Whoever we are
WE ARE KNOWN TO GOD

Whatever we've done
WE BELONG TO GOD

Wherever we go
WE ARE LOVED BY GOD

Every day, every moment
GOD IS OUR FRIEND

    When our way is joyful
    GOD WILL REJOICE WITH US

When the going is rough
GOD WILL WIPE AWAY OUR TEARS

We are God's people: we are held in love
OUR HOPE IS IN THE GOODNESS OF GOD

FIFTH SUNDAY OF EASTER

Cycle C

Acts 14:21–27; Ps 145; Rev 21:1–5; Jn 13:31–35

God is loving and full of kindness
GOD IS AT HOME IN US

God is welcoming and full of beauty
GOD IS AT HOME IN US

God is forgiving and full of justice
GOD IS AT HOME IN US

God is with us: we are God's people
GOD IS AT HOME IN US. AMEN

Day by day
As we have been loved
WE MUST LOVE EACH OTHER

Wherever we travel
As we have been loved
WE MUST LOVE EACH OTHER

All the way home
As we have been loved
WE MUST LOVE EACH OTHER

Our old life has ended
GOD IS MAKING US NEW

SIXTH SUNDAY OF EASTER

Cycle C

Acts 15:1–2, 22–29; Ps 67; Rev 21:10–14, 22–23; Jn 14:23–29

We come to a holy God
WE COME IN AWE AND WONDER

We come to a just God
WE COME TO ASK FOR HELP AND FORGIVENESS

We come to a loving God
WE COME SEEKING HELP AND A HUG

> Love God
> with everything that you have and are
> COME, HOLY SPIRIT
> REMIND US IN TRUTH
> WHAT JESUS SAID

> Love your neighbour
> as you love yourself
> COME, HOLY SPIRIT
> REMIND US EACH DAY
> WHAT JESUS SAID

> 'Do not be afraid:
> I am your friend and I love you'
> COME, HOLY SPIRIT
> REMIND US WITH JOY
> WHAT JESUS SAID

ASCENSION DAY

Cycle C, *see page 139*

SEVENTH SUNDAY OF EASTER

Cycle C

Acts 7:55–60; Ps 97; Rev 22:12–14, 16–17, 20; Jn 17:20–26

All who are hungry
COME AND EAT

All who are thirsty
COME AND DRINK

All who are weary
COME AND REST

All who are happy
COME AND SMILE

All who seek life and blessing
ARE WELCOME IN GOD'S HOUSE

> In the beginning
> GOD
>
> In the end
> GOD
>
> Moment by moment
> HOUR BY HOUR
>
> Day by day
> YEAR BY YEAR
>
> God is among us
> GOD IS WITHIN US
>
> First and last, Alpha and Omega,
> GOD IS GOD AND GOD LOVES US.

Ruth Burgess

TRINITY SUNDAY

Cycle C, *see page 201*

ASCENSION DAY

OPENING AND CLOSING RESPONSES FOR ASCENSION DAY

Cycles A, B and C

Acts 11:1–11; Ps 47; Eph 1:17–23; Mt 28:16–20 (Cycle A); Mk 16:15–20 (Cycle B); Lk 24:46–53 (Cycle C)

We know you and we do not know you
YOU ARE MYSTERIOUS AND FULL OF JOY

You know us and you understand us
YOU ARE LOVING AND FULL OF TRUTH

You welcome us and you live in us
YOU ARE HOLY AND FULL OF HOPE

We look for you in each other
WE LOOK FOR YOU IN OUR MIDST

Or:

What are you doing here?
WE ARE LOOKING FOR JESUS

What are you doing here?
WE HAVE QUESTIONS TO ASK

What are you doing here?
WE SEEK HOPE; WE SEEK HEALING

What are you doing here?
WE HAVE HEARD GOD CALLING OUR NAMES

Closing responses:

Cycle A

In the name of the Maker
WE GO

In the name of Jesus
WE GO

In the name of the Holy Spirit
WE GO

We go in wonder
WE GO IN HOPE AND LOVE

Cycle B

We go in hope
TO LIVE THE GOOD NEWS

We go in wonder
TO LIVE THE GOOD NEWS

We go in joy
TO LIVE THE GOOD NEWS

We go in the name of Jesus
IN THE SPIRIT'S WISDOM AND IN THE FRIENDSHIP OF GOD. AMEN

Cycle C

GOD OF LAUGHTER AND TEARS,
IMMERSE US IN GLORY,
CLOTHE US WITH POWER,
FILL US WITH WISDOM,
BLESS US WITH LOVE. AMEN

Ruth Burgess

IN A CLOUD

In a cloud.
A cloud?
A bit dramatic wasn't it, Jesus?
A bit over the top!

Hands raised.
Floating heavenwards ......
And I'll lay odds that
future artists
will dress you in shining white,
and paint the sky deep blue –
to 'match' your eyes.
OK – so there were some precedents:
Elijah and his chariots
and that fiery cloudy pillar thing that moved around the wilderness;
but those were the old ways –
you aren't like that.

Is this really what you want us to remember about you, Jesus?
That you disappeared in a cloud
and that you now live somewhere above the skies,
way beyond our reach?

What about your stories, your friendship;
your tears, your pain, your laughter?

What about the way you believed in us,
trusted us,
sent us out to teach and heal?

I'm not sure that you being alive somewhere
where we cannot see you, talk with you,
laugh and cry with you,
is going to be much help to us, Jesus.

Please, can't you find a way of living with us,
close enough somehow for us to know that you're near?

You said something once about a Spirit,
a holy Spirit from God,
who would come to us.
Does that mean you're coming back to us?

And if you are –
no dramatics this time, please Jesus.
Just come back to us quietly ...
No more clouds!

Ruth Burgess

A PRAYER FOR ASCENSION DAY

Let us give thanks
for all the signs of the Lordship of Jesus
in our world today:

For Christian men and women
offering themselves for election to public office;
for those who serve Christ
in the civil service
and other fields of public service;
for all who seek to walk Christ's way
in the world of business, commerce,
and industry;
for those who seek to honour Jesus
in the caring professions.
They seek to honour Christ;
AND WE HONOUR THEM.

For congregations quietly working
to welcome refugees and asylum-seekers;
for men and women of faith
struggling to overcome the debts of nations
in order to feed the nations' starving people
and to house the nations' homeless ones;
for Christian teachers, parents and youth workers,
celebrating the Kingdom amongst the young;
for carers; and for old people
facing the end of one stage of the journey,
approaching in faith the next.
They seek to honour Christ;
AND WE HONOUR THEM.

John Harvey

ASCENSION INTERCESSIONS

The Ascension speaks to us of the reign of Christ and his Kingdom; that theme informs these intercessions.

Instead of the spoken response, a sung response could be used, such as 'Through our lives and by our prayers' (John L. Bell and Graham Maule, Come All You People, *Wild Goose Publications)*

Let us hold before God all those whom Christ calls to follow him –
when faith is great and when faith is little;
when faith is sure and when faith clings by its fingernails;
when faith sees clearly and when faith gropes;
when faith reassures and when faith challenges;
when following is easy and when following brings conflict –
both those who follow Christ with firm tread and those whose step is less steady –
that, among God's people, joys may be celebrated and tears may be shed,
all are welcomed, young and old, seeker and stranger,
God's Kingdom is both sought and lived,
and the Good News of Jesus Christ is shared and proclaimed.

Your Kingdom come.
YOUR WILL BE DONE.

Let us hold before God all those to whom Christ offers his Kingdom:
the abused and the exploited;
the battered and the bruised;
the blind and the broken;
the deaf and the dumb;
the destitute and the dispirited;
the feeble and the forgotten;
the homeless and the hungry;
the lame and the lost;
the lonely and the unwelcome;
the outcast and the scapegoat;
the poor and the paralysed;
the sick and the sorrowful;
the unlovely and the unloved.

(Silence, or names and situations might be mentioned.)

Your Kingdom come.
YOUR WILL BE DONE.

Let us bring to God those conditions in which we long to see Christ reign:
where conflict is a reality and peace but a dream;
where greed is honoured and generosity is mocked;
where injustice reigns and justice is trampled underfoot;
where the powerful are heard and the powerless are ignored;
where people are discriminated against because of race, creed and gender.
where the earth is abused;
where historic hate lives;
where honest work is derided or denied.

(Silence, or names and situations might be mentioned.)

Your Kingdom come.
YOUR WILL BE DONE.

Give to us, O God,
A VISION OF YOUR KINGDOM,
A GLIMPSE OF YOUR GLORY,
AN OPENNESS TO YOUR RULE,
AND YOUR SPIRIT TO GUIDE US.
HEAR US, WE PRAY, THROUGH CHRIST,
THE RISEN AND ASCENDED ONE.
AMEN

David Hamflett

LET US CELEBRATE

Instead of the spoken version here, any sung setting of the Sanctus could be used.

Look, here is bread!
Look, here is wine!
LET US CELEBRATE THE FEAST OF GOD!

Lift up your hearts.
WE LIFT THEM TO THE LORD.
Let us give thanks to the Lord our God.
IT IS RIGHT TO GIVE OUR THANKS AND PRAISE.

To you ...
Creator God, who spoke the universe into being through your Word,
who formed us in your own image,
who called us by name,
to you we lift our hearts
AND GIVE OUR THANKS AND PRAISE.

To you ...
Redeeming God, who was born as one of us in Jesus,
who told stories, restored the lost and broken, and broke barriers,
who died and rose for us, and lives and reigns for ever,
to you we lift our hearts
AND GIVE OUR THANKS AND PRAISE.

To you...
Sustaining God, who is ever-present with us through the Holy Spirit,
who calls us, leads us, inspires and upholds us,
who brings us into a fellowship beyond earthly ties,
to you we lift our hearts
AND GIVE OUR THANKS AND PRAISE.

And now we join our voices with those of your people of every time and place
    as we praise you with the song of heaven:

HOLY, HOLY, HOLY LORD,
GOD OF POWER AND MIGHT.
HEAVEN AND EARTH ARE FULL OF YOUR GLORY.

HOSANNA IN THE HIGHEST.
BLESSED IS HE WHO COMES IN THE NAME OF THE LORD.
HOSANNA IN THE HIGHEST.

Before he parted from his friends,
Jesus prepared a last supper to share with them.
He took some bread, and gave thanks for it.
Then he broke it and gave it to them.
'Take and eat; this is my body,' he said.
When supper was all but over,
he took a cup of wine,
gave thanks for it, and gave it to them to drink.
'This cup is the new relationship with God,
sealed with my blood.
Take and drink from it. It is for all.'

Ascension Christ,
In the breaking of bread and the pouring of wine,
COME TO US.
As we do now what you once did on earth,
BE PRESENT WITH US.
Breathe your Spirit upon this bread and wine.
MAY THEY BECOME OUR SPIRITUAL FOOD AND DRINK.
Breathe your Spirit upon us.
MAY WE BE YOUR BODY, REVEALING YOUR PRESENCE IN THE WORLD. AMEN

David Hamflett

HELP US TO SEE

'Why do you stand looking up towards heaven?' (Acts 1:10–11a)

We look for you,
straining our eyes
into the far country,
but our vision is disrupted
by the least, the lost,
the littlest, the last
among us.

We race after you,
trying to catch up,
and turning the corner
find only
a homeless family
in our path.

We wander the streets,
yearning to find you,
calling your name,
but it is only

a single mother who turns
and wearily smiles,

a street person
who whispers 'hello',

a little girl who pirouettes
and takes our hand.

Gone ...

But you are still here, Lord.
Help us to see.

Thom M. Shuman

PENTECOST

OPENING AND CLOSING RESPONSES FOR PENTECOST SUNDAY

Cycles A, B and C

Acts 2:1–11; Ps 104; 1 Cor 12:3–7, 12–13; Jn 20:19–23

God speaks to us
IN THE RICHES OF CREATION

God speaks to us
IN THE STORIES OF JESUS

God speaks to us
IN THE LIVES OF OTHER PEOPLE

God speaks to us
IN WORDS AND WAYS THAT WE CAN UNDERSTAND

    God of fire and beauty
    WARM US

    God of peace and justice
    DISTURB US

    God of wind and wonder
    AMAZE US

    God of Pentecost
    KINDLE YOUR LOVE IN OUR LIVES

Ruth Burgess

OPENING RESPONSES FOR A PENTECOST SERVICE

God says: I will pour out my Spirit on all people.
THE SPIRIT HAS COME. ALLELUIA!

Christ says: I will ask the Father
and he will give you another Counsellor to be with you for ever.
THE SPIRIT HAS COME. ALLELUIA!

Come, Holy Spirit, gentle as a dove,
burning as fire,
powerful as the wind.
COME, HOLY SPIRIT, COME.

David Hamflett

THE SURPRISING THING ABOUT PENTECOST

What?

Who's there?

Oh, it's you.

Yes – the Teacher told me you would be coming round. I was waiting for you and must have dozed off.

Now, let me see. You want to know what happened on that day. Oh, it was so long ago.

Of course, you've come to the right person. A lot of folk will tell you they were in the city that day. But I was a lifelong resident of Jerusalem – in fact, my house was right next door to where Peter, James, John and all the rest used to gather for their meetings.

That fact alone surprised a lot of us. I mean, the followers of Jesus staying in the very city where he had been put to death!

Not that they caused any trouble, mind you. They obviously weren't the band of zealots that everyone had thought – or hoped – they would be. If they were up to something in that city, the authorities would have known about it pretty quick, let me tell you. Between the Roman spies, Herod, and the council of priests, you never knew who was watching you.

Anyway, it was Pentecost.

Nowadays, everyone associates it with this new faith: the great day when the Church was born.

But people forget that we Jews have been celebrating Pentecost for a very long time. First it was an agricultural festival – to celebrate the first harvest of the year and to give thanks for God's blessing. Over the years, though, it became more a celebration of God's gift of the Law to the people.

Each year, thousands of Jews from all over the region returned to Jerusalem to celebrate their religious heritage – to dance, to sing, to reminisce, to gather together for worship in the Temple.

So, it was not all that surprising that there were so many people around that day, so many excited people, so many people eager to rejoice and party.

Peter and the others – oh, there were probably only a hundred of them at most – had gathered at the house to pray and worship together.

No – not *that* house. The authorities had torn down the original.

Where was I?

Right ... Anyway, they were praying and worshipping – I could hear them through the open windows – when, suddenly, there was the strangest sound.

First, it was just a hint, a whisper of a breeze.

Then the wind raced down the streets, rushing past the houses, sounding like a thousand chariots coming at us.

One of the neighbours later said it sounded like the first day of creation must have sounded when God breathed upon the earth and the waters.

I tell you, I dropped my tools and ran out into the street – just like everyone else.

Huh?

Of course we were surprised!

Actually, most of us were pretty frightened. I've never heard a noise like it since that day, and quite frankly I hope I never will.

Then I heard someone shout: 'Look at the house!' meaning the house where Jesus's people were.

The doors and the windows were wide open – we could see in quite clearly.

How can I describe it?

It looked as if flames – tongues of fire is what Luke called them later, I think – were dancing about the room. At first I thought the cooking oil had caught fire and exploded. But then I noticed that nothing was burning ... and that no one – I mean NO ONE – in the house was hysterical or even frightened. No, they just stood and watched as the flames filled the room; and the flames seemed to touch – without burning them – every single person in that house.

It was an incredible sight!

We were rubbing our eyes, pinching ourselves, looking at one another in wonder and fear.

Then – the words came.

I think it was Peter at first, but then John, and then someone else, and then another, until all the disciples – every single person in that house – were talking and chattering away.

A man in back of me shouted: 'They must be drunk!'

But a man standing near me said: 'No. I understand what he's saying. He's speaking a Mede dialect.'

A rabbi corrected him. 'No, my son, that's Aramaic.'

I heard a woman mutter under her breath, 'Men! It's clearly Egyptian they are speaking.'

Me, I'm no good at languages. It was all Greek to me.

But everybody – and I mean everybody – Roman, Jew, Turk, Cyrenian, Galilean, all the different nationalities that were standing there in the street – heard – each in his or her native tongue – what the followers of Jesus were saying.

It was an awesome display of power and majesty. I felt like one of the ancient Israelites must have felt when God spoke to Moses from the mountaintop, in thunder and lightning.

Well, you know the rest.

Peter came out of the house and spoke to all the people standing in the street. He had a quiet crowd – believe me.

What a sight: This uneducated fisherman speaking to a crowd composed of every race and nation in the world.

You know, some say the Church was born on that day. Others say it was the day that the Holy Spirit came down.

Me, I think it was the day Peter became the person God intended him to be.

What a speech – so simple but powerful.

It was so overwhelming that 3,000 people were baptised into the faith!

Yes, it was a day of incredible drama, a day of miracles, a day in which lives were changed ...

What? Sorry?

What surprised me most?

The most surprising thing about Pentecost was that the disciples WERE NOT SURPRISED!

I mean, the wind didn't scare them, the flames didn't panic them, the crowds didn't intimidate them.

It was as if they expected it all to happen to them: the rush of wind, the touch of the flames, the speaking in tongues, the powerful sermon, the response of the people.

It was as if someone had told them ahead of time that, if they only trusted, if they only believed, if they only had faith, it would happen just like it did.

Thom M. Shuman

A PRAYER FOR PENTECOST

Spirit of God,
flickering over our heads,
illuminating our faces,
inspiring our thoughts,
give us now, we pray,
WORDS OF JOY AND PRAISE.

Spirit of God,
filling our hearts with hope,
steadying our nerves with peace,
comforting our lives with love,
give us now, we pray,
WORDS OF JOY AND PRAISE.

Spirit of God,
come to us now –
surging through the darkness of our lives,
sweeping over our weariness –

so that, in this time of Pentecost,
the sparkling light of faith,
the rushing wind of hope
and the joyful sound of praise
may echo round the world,
may echo in the church,
and find their response in us.
Spirit of God, give us now, we pray,
WORDS OF JOY AND PRAISE. AMEN

John Harvey

AN AFFIRMATION FOR PENTECOST

We believe in a loving God,
whose Word sustains our lives
and the work of our hands in the world.

GOD IS LIFE.

We believe in God's Son amongst us,
sowing the seed of life's renewal.
He lived with the poor
to show the meaning of love.

JESUS CHRIST IS LORD.

We believe in the Holy Spirit of Life,
making us one with God,
renewing our strength with Her own.

THE SPIRIT IS LOVE.

John Harvey

FIRE SONGS

Flame of candle flickering softly,
heralding the dawning day,
singing songs of hope and promise,
keeping night and fear at bay.

Hearth fire embers red and glowing,
quickly fanned into a flame,
speak of warmth and love and shelter,
tell of life restored again.

Beacon fires leaping skyward:
song of war on hilltop borne;
cries for justice, peace and freedom,
look towards a better dawn.

Volcano fires bursting outwards,
who can their awesome power view?
All-devouring, all-destroying,
shaking old, creating new.

Lightning splits the paths of heaven –
judgement fire, when all must bow
as the skies are torn asunder
and all things fulfilled below.

Long ago, Your people knew it:
fire descending from above,
singing judgement, singing freedom,
singing life and singing love.

Songs of healing, songs of sorrow,
songs for old and songs for young,
songs of mercy and compassion
are the songs the fires sung.

Fire consuming, not destroying,
fire that beckons home the lost;
all these things and more, You gave us
when You came at Pentecost.

Alix Brown

WHEN THE DAY OF PENTECOST CAME

(This prayer could be read by two voices.)

When the day of Pentecost came there was a noise … like a strong wind blowing.

Wind to blow away the cobwebs of our tradition.
Wind to freshen our faces and awaken us to the challenges of today.
Wind to fill our sails and send us on a voyage of spiritual discovery.

Wind of the Spirit,
blow strongly through the Church
and enliven us with the breath of God.

They saw … tongues of fire …

Fire to burn away the rubbish in our lives.
Fire for spiritual heat to 'strangely warm' our hearts.
Fire to light a beacon of hope for the people in our communities.

Fire of the Spirit,
blaze away in the Church
and set us on fire for the Gospel.

They heard the believers speaking in their own languages.

Speaking in a way that people can understand.
Speaking to real needs, having something to say on real issues.
Speaking so that our neighbours want to listen.

Words of the Spirit,
speak to us and through us,
that we may preach the living Word.

But others said: 'These people are drunk!'

Perhaps they were:
Drunk on the new wine of the Kingdom of God.
High on the power of the Holy Spirit –
celebrating the birth of the Church of Jesus Christ.

Holy Spirit of God,
inspire and excite us as we celebrate in worship,
and empower the work and witness of your Church today. Amen

David Lemmon

COME, HOLY SPIRIT

Music based on a Spiritual
Arrangement and words: Carol Dixon

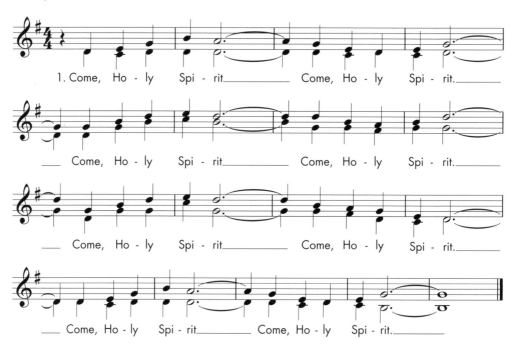

2nd time:
Bring us to Jesus

3rd time:
Grant us God's peace

Final time:
Come, Holy Spirit,
Bring us to Jesus,
Grant us God's peace.
Come, Holy Spirit.

Note: This song works best like this: 1st time melody only, 2nd time bring in the lower part, 3rd and 4th times bring in the instruments.

ON THE GREAT DAY OF PENTECOST

On the great day of Pentecost, a mighty wind surged forth from heaven, pushing the followers of Jesus out of the house where they had been hiding, and into the streets. Flames danced above their heads, their tongues began to wag, and people from all over the world heard what they said – no matter what their native language.

Peter gave a sermon which would cause Billy Graham to turn green with envy – and three thousand people were baptised.

The Church of Jesus Christ was born!

On the day *after* Pentecost:

Peter's wife had to yell at him three times to get out of bed, so that he would get his sermon on the website before 9:00 am.

The deacons grumbled about cleaning out the baptismal pool.

And the apostles argued about who got to preach on Trinity Sunday, who would choose the hymns, and who would be stuck chairing the Nominating Committee.

Come, Holy Spirit, with your gracious language.
Come, Holy Spirit, with your passion for all people.
Come, Holy Spirit, with your uniting peace.

Come, Holy Spirit!

Thom M. Shuman

HOLY SPIRIT MEDITATION

Who is this Holy Spirit?
Sounds a bit spooky to me!
Weren't those weird old prophets
meant to be Spirit-filled? –
and a lot of strange things they did!
And what about King David
dancing before the Lord and all that? –
his wife was appalled.
Then at Pentecost some odd things happened:
'Speaking in tongues'
and everyone hearing in their own language –
little wonder people thought the disciples were drunk.
No, you'll not catch me
having anything to do with the Holy Spirit.
I mean, Christianity is meant to be
safe and sensible, isn't it?
Who needs the Holy Spirit?

Carol Dixon

THE GIFT OF YOURSELF

Intercessions for Whitsunday

We praise you, O God,
FOR YOUR WONDERFUL GIFT OF YOURSELF.

Spirit of the Living God,
from Holy Wisdom brooding on the waters of creation
to the Spirit with us now and enabling us to worship,
you have been gently and powerfully at work in our history.

We praise you, O God,
FOR YOUR WONDERFUL GIFT OF YOURSELF.

Spirit of the Living God,
breathing life into all that lives and loves,

inspiring work and choices, guiding and moulding,
you are still gently and powerfully at work in our world.

We praise you, O God,
FOR YOUR WONDERFUL GIFT OF YOURSELF.

Spirit of the Living God,
from knitting us together in our mother's wombs
to embracing us while we draw our last breaths,
you are gently and powerfully at work in our lives.

We praise you, O God,
FOR YOUR WONDERFUL GIFT OF YOURSELF.

Spirit of the Living God,
we ask for your holding particularly of these whom we name now:
(names of those who are sick)

We ask your comfort for those who mourn, especially the family and friends of:
(names of those who are deceased)

Spirit of the Living God,
fall afresh on us,
freshen us, renew us,
open our eyes to the needful tasks
and our own abilities to fulfil the work.

Enable us to be identified as God's holy people
by our love and joy,
our peace and patience,
our kindness and generosity,
our faithfulness, gentleness and self-control.
May we shine as lights in the world to the glory of God.

We praise you, O God,
FOR YOUR WONDERFUL GIFT OF YOURSELF.
AMEN

Liz Knowles

PRAYERS OF INTERCESSION FOR PENTECOST

Spirit of fire,
inflame in us a passion for justice and equality:
THAT WE MAY KNOW THE CLEANSING OF OUR PREJUDICES AND FEARS
AND PROCLAIM YOUR FREEDOM BOLDLY,
CARESSING YOUR EARTH WITH HUMILITY.

Spirit of compassion,
infuse us with your longings for wholeness and happiness:
THAT WE MAY REACH OUT TO THOSE WHO ARE HURTING AND DISORDERED,
ENFOLDING ONE ANOTHER WITH YOUR LOVE AND TENDERNESS.

Spirit of wisdom,
be within us in our journeying, gently guiding us along right paths:
THAT WE MAY BE LED TOWARDS TRANSFORMATION AND NEW BEGINNINGS
IN OUR WORLD.

Spirit of gentleness,
touch us anew, releasing in us all that we are afraid of:
THAT WE MAY KNOW YOUR ACCEPTANCE OF US,
AND FREELY ACCEPT AND EMBRACE OTHERS.

Spirit of power,
hold us in our powerlessness:
THAT WE MAY KNOW YOUR STRENGTH AND BECOME A VOICE FOR THE VOICELESS,
HEALING FOR THE WOUNDED
AND EMPOWERMENT FOR THE WEAK.

Spirit of judgement,
be tender with us and show us your mercy:
THAT WE MAY HUMBLY LEARN OF YOU
AND NOT BE AFRAID TO BE YOUR PROPHETS IN THE WORLD.

Spirit of comfort,
draw near to us in all grief, confusion and pain;
in your graciousness, bring hope, consolation and renewal:
THAT MANY MAY LOOK UP
AND DISCOVER YOU IN THE MIDST.

Spirit of dance,
be our playfulness:
THAT WE MAY LEAP AND LAUGH AND ENTER YOUR JOY.
GIVE US CONFIDENCE IN LIFE AND ASSURANCE IN DEATH.

Elizabeth Baxter

PENTECOST PRAYER

Holy, sprightly Spirit of God,
we delight at your dancing among us,
filling the world with joyful possibility,
revealing the music of the Creator.
We rejoice at your daring spontaneity
and find ourselves caught off guard by your unexpected communications.

In a world that can seem predictable,
you spark into being new possibilities:
you gently purge our sin in the warmth of your breath,
freeing us from our bondage to past wrong.

In a world that can seem drab,
you weave your ever-changing patterns into the fabric of our beings.

In a world that can be hostile,
your mediating love builds a path from loneliness to conviviality,
from antagonism to co-operation.

In a world that can appear purposeless,
your vitality shouts out a mighty 'Yes' to life
and declares the source of all living to be the One from whom you proceed,
the Father and Mother, Creator and Lover of all.

We make our prayer in the name of Jesus, who promised your coming
and reigns with you in the eternal fellowship of the Creator,
one perfect Trinity of love. Amen

John McLuckie

A MEDITATION FOR PENTECOST

She sits like a bird, brooding on the waters,
hovering on the chaos of the world's first day;
she sighs and she sings, mothering creation,
waiting to give birth to all the Word will say. ⋆

Sitting. Waiting. Here we are, sitting, waiting. Silently we take in the noises and the movements around us (some can be named: the wind, the cars, the cries of children …). We listen to the beat of our own hearts, to the breeze of our breath moving – in – out – in – out, feeding, nourishing our bodies. We sense others around us. We are aware of the shape of the room, of the feel of the chair holding us. We can sense the light from the windows. And we are aware of our own bodies, full and beautiful, living and relating, created by God for our pleasure.

We sit and we wait. And in our sitting, we hover, we brood – never quite settled, never quite still, always perched, ready to move – to move by the power of breath in our bodies. To move with the power of the Holy Spirit dwelling in us.

(silence)

She wings over earth, resting where she wishes,
lighting close at hand or soaring through the skies;
she nests in the womb, welcoming each wonder,
nourishing potential hidden to our eyes.

Nourishment. Food. Sustenance – reaching deep down and reviving us. Where are you most deeply nourished? Where do you feel most energy flooding into your body and soul? In the quiet moments of the early morning? In the weary rest of the late evening? On the top of a high mountain? In the company of good friends? Perhaps it is when you are listening to good music, or when you go for a long walk and are aware of the sounds and the smells and the sights that you would normally take for granted. Or maybe it is when you are browsing in a bookshop. Wherever you feel nourished, drawn out unexpectedly and refreshed, there the Spirit is moving.

(silence)

She dances in fire, startling her spectators,
waking tongues of ecstasy where dumbness reigned;
she weans and inspires all whose hearts are open,
nor can she be captured, silenced or restrained.

She was certainly not to be restrained this particular evening. She staggered in from her home on the streets into our worship in the church centre with her mate, both of them weaving and dodging each other in their drunken haze. She had red, fiery hair; a long tweed coat; a plastic handbag draped over her crooked arm and a plaster cast on her left leg. As she stumbled in, startling the worshippers, we were singing 'Lord of the Dance'. When we got to the line, 'they cut me down and I leapt up high' – she came alive. Her arms shot into the air, she whooped as if about to 'strip the willow', and SHE DANCED, while we sang. She danced for us; she celebrated her bruised and battered body. And for those few minutes her whole body smiled. She was a wild woman. A wild dancer filled with the Spirit. We didn't exchange words. We didn't muddle ourselves with borrowed language. We spoke in smiles, and twirls and whoops and yelps – in tongues of ecstasy.

(silence)

For she is the Spirit, one with God in essence,
gifted by the Saviour in eternal love;
she is the key opening the scriptures,
enemy of apathy and heavenly dove.

She is the Spirit, Ruach, Sophia, Wisdom, the creator of the Word. She is with us always, opening our eyes, dancing in our hearts, wooing us to the words of God. She is eternal love. She is the key, the channel, the wind and the fire, the way ahead and the comfort all around. She is the graceful, peaceful dove enfolding us in her love. And she is the disturbing, enraging wild goose never allowing us to become lazy, always cajoling us on to new love and life. She is the enemy of apathy.

Ruth Harvey

*All verses from the song 'Enemy of Apathy', by John L. Bell and Graham Maule, Enemy of Apathy, *Wild Goose Publications*

COME AMONG US

Come, Holy Spirit.
Come, loving Jesus.
Come, glorious God.
Come among us and hallow our prayers:

We pray for the places in our world where there is poverty, fear and war.
May all who recognise your name hear you calling them to be peacemakers,
God, in your mercy,
HEAR OUR PRAYER.

We pray for young Christians – young in years, young in faith.
May the faith we pass on to them be a reflection
of the work of your Holy Spirit in our lives.
God, in your mercy.
HEAR OUR PRAYER.

We pray for our local churches.
May all who meet together to celebrate this Pentecost
experience your presence and be filled with power and joy.
God, in your mercy,
HEAR OUR PRAYER.

We pray for those who are ill, or in trouble, or in any kind of need.
We pray for those who have died, for those who are safe in your love.
God, in your mercy,
HEAR OUR PRAYER.

We pray for ourselves, our hopes, our questions, our needs, our dreams:
Come, holy and life-giving Spirit, renew our lives with love.
God, in your mercy,
HEAR OUR PRAYER.

Bright God of life,
burn in our lives,
blow us clean and holy,
warm us with courage and joy,
keep us in the mystery of your glory
all the days of our journey home.
Amen

Ruth Burgess

COME, HOLY SPIRIT

I have to admit that I have never had any tongues of fire dancing on my head. Though, come to think of it, there was that time when I was in the children's choir at a Christmas Eve service, when the lighted candle in the hand of the little girl behind me got too close to the hair on the back of my head! (But I'm not sure if that counts.)

I don't recall my folks mentioning anything about a white dove appearing at my baptism and a voice speaking from heaven.

Even though there were several wild geese flying over me on this morning's walk, I apparently don't have the spiritual gift to discern what they're saying.

But there are those times when Paisley curls up in my lap after a long day, and starts purring, when I feel the healing presence of the Comforter.

And in the middle of the night, when I hear my wife, Bonnie, softly breathing next to me, I am filled with a peace that is impossible to describe.

And this morning – like every other morning – the Holy Spirit bounded up onto the bed and started licking my face, saying, 'Come on; get up, lazy bones! Let's go see what God has in store for us today!'

Come, Holy Spirit, come!

Thom M. Shuman

GOD OF FIRE

God of fire, burn brightly in your Church.
Consume our petty concerns and jealousies,
purify our deeds and intentions,
kindle in our hearts the fire of your love.
Amen

David Hamflett

SUDDEN FROM OUT THE AIR

(Tune: Moscow)

Sudden from out the air
to those becalmed in care
blows wild the wind:
with strong and powerful sound,
with dancing fire around,
the Spirit comes to ground
in every mind.

Spirit of then and now,
teach us, your people, how
to wait on you;
send now your living fire;
our minds and hearts inspire,
that we may never tire
on the way true.

Explode in power and light
upon the darkened sight
of each and all;
unblock our deafened ear,
remove our cautious fear,
among your people here
awake your call.

Send us out to the street,
where people pass and meet,
with words to say
of freedom and release,
of hope and love and peace:
through us may you increase
Christ's living way.

Leith Fisher

HOLY SPIRIT

ON EVERYONE WHO LOOKS TO GOD

Words and melody: Ian M. Fraser
Arrangement: Douglas Galbraith

1. On ev - 'ry-one who looks to God, on ev - 'ry-one the Spi - rit falls, en-fold - ing in her wide em-brace all types who make the hu - man race, dis-tri - but - ing the gifts of grace,_ break-ing di - vid - ing walls:_ on ev - 'ry-one, on ev - 'ry-one, on ev - 'ry-one who looks to God, on ev - 'ry-one who looks to God the_en - abl - ing Spi - rit falls._

25

O'er everyone who looks to God,
o'er everyone the Spirit bends,
to stretch our minds and spirits till,
in Christ's full stature growing still,
we live in him and do his will,
finding he calls us friends:
for everyone, for everyone,
for everyone who looks to God,
for everyone who looks to God,
there's growth that never ends.

MYSTERIOUS GOD

Mysterious God,
you rustle the trees
and rattle my soul
and put paid to my feelings of aloneness.

You tap a march
up the spine of my being,
crash into doubt
and cast fear down
where fear belongs.

The shadow of death
is but a shadow,
for life's spark is lit
by your Spirit of love.

Alma Fritchley

FREE FLOWING SPIRIT

Free flowing Spirit
gather my loved ones

travel with them

dance with them

lift their spirits

that they may
find their strength

their confidence

their freedom

in you
the ground of their being

Elizabeth Baxter

O HOLY SPIRIT

(Tune: Christe Sanctorum)

O Holy Spirit, power of God's creation,
hope of the world, the Christians' inspiration,
spark deep within us fires of re-creation;
Spirit, renew us.

Creative Spirit, wake us to each other;
with your caresses touch us as a lover
that in your presence we may hold each other;
Spirit, renew us.

O Holy Spirit – in your life awaking,
our life hid in you, in your power partaking –
let your transforming breath, our torpor shaking,
come and renew us.

Come then, O Spirit, help us share the vision
of all creation healed of its division,
in God united and in Christ forgiven;
Spirit, renew us.

David Fox

GOD'S WHISPER

A rap of knuckles on the door:
welcome promise of company.
Winter's sleet tapping for attention
on my bedroom window.
Starlings squabbling,
truculent and noisy
on a branch
against a darkening sky.
A poke in the ribs!
A tap on the funny bone.
A lover's caress,
her soft, minty breath on my cheek.
Sun-baked wind in my hair,
the sand so hot against chill English feet.
And a dream, barely grasped,
launching me, laughing, out of sleep.
Your Spirit speaks to me
in mysterious ways.

Alma Fritchley

VISITING MY NANA

I recall as a child visiting my nana, who was close to the end of her life on earth. She had been bedridden for years, and had become frail, and so tiny in her bed. I can still see her smiling face and hear her frail voice singing one of Sankey's hymns – it was for me a holy moment, as if the very gates of heaven had opened up, and God had come down among us. Time has erased the words she gave me that day long ago, but the message remains: I was always to pass the faith on to others.

It was many years before the power of her words were to shape my daily life … I have found, so often in my life, that just the thought of that moment puts fire into my faith, hope into my heart and joy into my soul. Is not this the way the Holy Spirit, the go-between God, as he is called, comes to us again and again, and meets us with his liberating grace and power, and puts hope in our lives and peace in our hearts?

Written in a workshop on Iona, 1986, author unknown

LITANY OF THE SPIRIT

This piece works very well when read over background music. We use the Taizé chant
Veni, Creator Spiritus but any meditative piece of music would work.

God of all beginnings
God of endings
Eternal light of God
Warm breath of God
Melting touch of God
Healing hand of God
Creative love of God
Life-loving Spirit
Breath of the universe
Craftsman of the heavens
Star-kindling Spirit
Sun-warming Spirit
Moon-burnishing Spirit
Bud-bursting Spirit
Sap-surging Spirit
Painter of rainbows
Craftsman of trees
Artist of flowers
Midwife of creatures
Source of all life
Spirit of justice
Spirit of righteousness
Spirit of power
Spirit of integrity
Spirit of mercy
Spirit of compassion
Spirit of perfection
Spirit of generosity
Spirit of invitation
Spirit of spirit of gladness
Spirit of exuberance
Spirit of hope without horizon
Light of our lives
Supporter in our trials
Strength in weakness
Consolation in grief

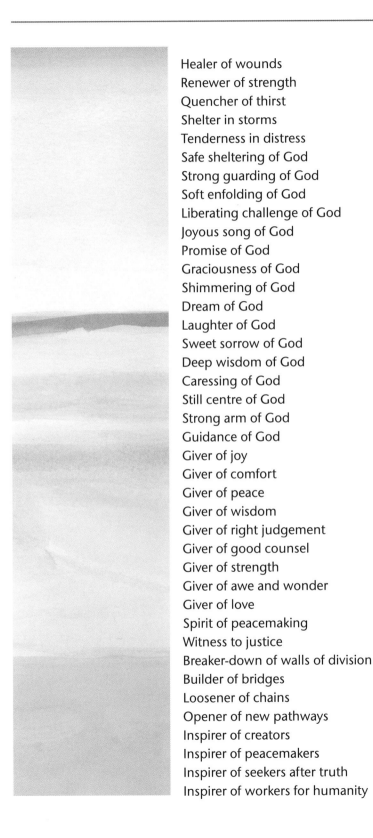

Healer of wounds
Renewer of strength
Quencher of thirst
Shelter in storms
Tenderness in distress
Safe sheltering of God
Strong guarding of God
Soft enfolding of God
Liberating challenge of God
Joyous song of God
Promise of God
Graciousness of God
Shimmering of God
Dream of God
Laughter of God
Sweet sorrow of God
Deep wisdom of God
Caressing of God
Still centre of God
Strong arm of God
Guidance of God
Giver of joy
Giver of comfort
Giver of peace
Giver of wisdom
Giver of right judgement
Giver of good counsel
Giver of strength
Giver of awe and wonder
Giver of love
Spirit of peacemaking
Witness to justice
Breaker-down of walls of division
Builder of bridges
Loosener of chains
Opener of new pathways
Inspirer of creators
Inspirer of peacemakers
Inspirer of seekers after truth
Inspirer of workers for humanity

Inspirer of children
Inspirer of mystics

Wellspring of life
Fresh spring of renewal
Clear stream of refreshment
Wide ocean of love

Divine wind, Breath of God,
as a whisper on the breeze,
a wind dancing in the treetops,
an exhilarating wind of the clifftops,

so we sense You.

Wellspring

LIKE A WILD BIRD

A baptismal hymn
(Tune: Sursum Corda)

Like a wild bird, out of the air so clear,
the Spirit comes down by the water's side,
sure and eternal sign that God is near;
in Christ baptised, God ever will abide.

Like a bright fire and mighty rushing wind,
the Spirit comes and faith is born again;
the truth is heard in every heart and mind;
Christ is proclaimed in accents clear and plain.

We bring our gifts of faith before your face;
Lord, now among us your same Spirit send.
Confirm in us the knowledge of your grace
and set us on the way that knows no end.

Enfold this child within your bonds of love;
kindle faith's flame in those who hold her/him dear;
and in our life together may we prove
the presence of your Spirit ever near.

Leith Fisher

REJOICE! O DAUGHTER OF ZION

The feminine imagery in this poem reflects the ancient Hebrew concept of the Spirit of God as feminine.

Rejoice! Rejoice, O Daughter of Zion.
Rejoice that you are a woman,
a daughter of Zion!

Delight in the person you are,
made in the image of God.
Woven together in your mother's womb
by the master weaver,
bearing the image of God in your womanhood.
Rejoice! Rejoice, O Daughter of Zion.

Delight in the complexity of who you are.
The complex structure of your body.
The intricacies of emotion and personality.
The delicate balance of your body, mind and spirit.
The whole image woven in the image of God.
Rejoice! Rejoice, O Daughter of Zion.

Rejoice! Rejoice, O Daughter of Zion,
that it is the Spirit of God alive in you.
The Spirit of God who is the lifter of your head,
who adorns you with beauty and grace.
It is her Spirit you bear.
Her Spirit who empowers you as a partner in the work of God.

Rejoice! Rejoice, O Daughter of Zion.
Rejoice and delight in your womanhood.
Rejoice greatly, O Daughter of Zion!

Anne Lawson

WALKING WITH THE HOLY SPIRIT

We walk together,
you and I,
talking sometimes,
often in an awesome silence.
Wandering and wondering with you,
Holy Spirit,
unrestrained as the wild winds,
ever-moving as the tides.
Fire of passion.
Still small voice.

Frances Hawkey

LORD GOD, WHOSE SPIRIT DRIVES US OUT

(Tune: Sussex Carol)

Lord God, whose Spirit drives us out
beyond convention's rules and laws
to walk on water for your cause
and test what faith is all about,
nerve us for risks the Spirit asks,
strange venturing and daunting tasks.

Lord God, whose Spirit advocates
structure and form which will endure
that generations may secure
gains which past faithfulness creates,
order our ways that we may find
order consistent with your mind.

Movement and institution weave
textures of life contrasting, strange,
yet open out the church to change
flexible life-forms to achieve:
firm boughs and moving sap combine
to make true branches of the Vine!

Ian M. Fraser

SAINTS' DAYS

BEING REMEMBERED

We all want to be remembered for something.

After developing an incredibly successful –
and controversial –
computer software company,
Bill Gates has announced
that he will donate 95% of his wealth to help people
throughout the world.

And people will remember him.

After taking vows to remain inside her cloistered convent,
Mother Teresa stepped
into the streets of Calcutta,
to serve the people of the world no one else wanted
to touch.

And people will remember her.

When it seemed that no one could break through
their set-in-stone ideas
about how to handle the problem,
rock star Bono turns out to be the one
who has convinced presidents and prime ministers to actually do something
concrete
about poverty in our world.

And people will remember.

We all want to be remembered for something.

This week, we are having our Vacation Bible School at church.
And three kids, so far, have come up to me and said:
'I remember you.
You're the guy we wrapped in toilet paper last year!'

Not exactly in the category of the others
but I'll take it!

Thom M. Shuman

A HYMN FOR ST DAVID'S DAY

(Tune: All Through the Night)

God, the source of all creation,
we sing your praise.
Lord of every land and nation,
we sing your praise.
For the treasures that you give us,
for the love you lavish on us,
for your Spirit dwelling in us,
we sing your praise.

For the saints who give you glory,
we give you thanks.
For the challenge of their story,
we give you thanks.
Thank you for St David's mission;
for his life and for his vision,
for his joy and dedication,
we give you thanks.

That our faith may shine more clearly,
dear Lord, we pray;
daily follow you more nearly,
dear Lord, we pray;
like St David to obey you,
by our lives bear witness to you
and together show we love you,
dear Lord, we pray.

Margaret Harvey

SAINTS ALIVE

(for St Beuno)

You lived,
so we are told,
so many years ago,
so long ago, indeed,
that now we seldom hear your name.

You lived,
and in beloved Wales,
land of your fathers,
you served your God –
you were a missioner for Christ.

You lived,
and, out of fierce dispute
over local land,
founded the Abbey
of Clynnog Fawr for Christ.

You lived,
and loved in guardian care,
dear Winefride, your niece,
and gave her life again
that others, too, might live.

You lived,
and in the Eastertide before your death
knew in your vision's eye
the glory and the joy
of Christ, risen for you.

You lived,
and for your missionary zeal
and loving care
you are recalled even now,
and April one and twenty is your day.

You lived –
but not just then
in Clynnog's cloistered walls,
amidst the grandeur of beloved Wales
and God's own people there.

You live –
you live even now –
for what you were
and what you then achieved live on
in our remembrances of you.

You live,
St Beuno,
saint of the Church;
when lives are hid in Christ,
saints are alive;
for this we now rejoice,
and always will.

Tom Gordon

LOVE IS GOD'S MEANING

A liturgy to celebrate the feast day of Julian of Norwich, 8th May

Give everyone a hazelnut or a pinecone as they enter the worship space.

Gathering

Loving God, you call us to marvel:
REVEAL IN US YOUR WONDER AND JOY.

Comforting God, you call us to gentleness:
REVEAL IN US YOUR PEACE AND FAITH.

Healing God, you call us to wholeness:
REVEAL IN US YOUR JUSTICE AND TRUTH.

As truly as God is our Father so God is our Mother:
REVEAL IN US LOVE AND CARE FOR ALL YOUR CREATION.

Song: Lord of life, CG (*Common Ground*) 76, CH4 (*Church Hymnary 4*) 782; or Sing to God with gladness, CG 112, CH4 150; or 'Tis a gift to be simple

Setting the scene

In 1373, a woman aged '30 and a half' was gravely ill. She and her family thought she was dying. But on 8th May she had a series of visions, which she referred to as her 'shewings', and which later became known as the *Revelations of Divine Love*. She became an anchoress, living in a cell attached to a church in Norwich from where she gave spiritual direction and lived a life of prayer. Julian's near-death experience made her value the wonder and joy in each moment and the gift of life that God gives us. Her writings shine through with compassion and love. Her message speaks beyond the Middle Ages and is as fresh today as when written:

'And in this Christ showed me a little thing the size of a hazelnut lying in the palm of my hand and it was as round as any ball. I looked there upon it with the eye of my understanding, and I thought: what may this be? And I was answered thus: it is all that is made. I marvelled how it might last, for I thought it might disintegrate to nothingness. And I was answered: it lasts and ever shall because God loves it, as have all things that have their being by the love of God. In this little thing I saw three properties: The first is that God made it, the second is that God loves it and the third is that God keeps it. When I behold the Maker, the Lover and the Keeper I know that I won't see true bliss unless I fully unite with God and rest in Him, with nought between us. That the knowledge I need is that God loves us and we should have love for God.' (from *The Revelations of Divine Love*, translation by Zam Walker)

Meditation

Leader: Take the hazelnut/pinecone and hold it in the palm of your hand. Marvel at the beauty and the intricacy of it. Look at the shape and the colours. Smell it. Take your time. Really examine it. Be fully present. This is 'all that is made'.

Bible reading: Luke 12:22–34 or Matthew 6:25–34

Song: A small thing like a hazelnut, CH4 142; or Look and learn, CG 72

Prayer

God-with-us, we pray for your creation.

FORGIVE US WHEN WE MISUSE RATHER THAN MARVEL,
WHEN WE CONSUME WITHOUT THOUGHT.

God-with-us, we pray for the world.
FORGIVE US WHEN WE DO NOT RECOGNISE THE NEIGHBOUR WHO LIVES BEYOND US,
WHEN WE IGNORE THE NEIGHBOUR WHO LIVES BESIDE US,
WHEN WE WANT POWER OVER RATHER THAN POWER WITH.

God-with-us, we pray for those who suffer:
For those who have life-limiting conditions.
For those who are near death ...
GRANT EACH OF US A REVELATION OF YOUR DIVINE LOVE
TO BUILD COMMUNITY AND MAKE YOUR BROKEN WORLD WHOLE. AMEN

Action of thanksgiving and commitment: *E.g. placing the hazelnuts/pinecones on a map of the world*

During the action a short song could be sung:

Mungu ni mwema, CH4 788; or Holy, holy, holy, CG 48, CH4 769; or In the Lord I'll be ever thankful, CH4 772

Affirmation

WE BELIEVE IN GOD:
A GOD OF LOVE AND RAINBOWS
WHO CREATES ALL THROUGH LOVE.
WHO PROMISES TO BE WITH CREATION IN SUN AND RAIN,
IN JOY AND PAIN.
WHO BLESSES US WITH WONDER IN EACH MOMENT
AND JOY IN EACH STEP.

WE BELIEVE IN GOD:
A GOD WHO WAS BORN IN JESUS.
WHO, IN SOLIDARITY, SUFFERS WITH US.
WHO KNEW DESPAIR AND LOSS AND BETRAYAL.
WHO WAS KILLED FOR STANDING UP FOR WHAT IS RIGHT
YET WHO SHOWED THAT LOVE IS STRONGER THAN DEATH.

WE BELIEVE IN GOD:
A GOD WHO IS GIFTED TO US IN THE SPIRIT.
WHO ENFOLDS AND UPHOLDS US.
WHO INSPIRES US WITH THE VISION OF HOW THINGS SHOULD BE.

WHO CHALLENGES US TO LIVE HONESTLY.
WHO TRANSFORMS OUR PAIN INTO NEW LIFE.
WHO EMPOWERS US WITH NEW BEGINNINGS.

WE BELIEVE IN GOD:
A GOD OF LOVE AND LAUGHTER
WHO CALLS US TO LIVE TODAY IN JUSTICE AND JOY
IN THE KNOWLEDGE THAT
ALL SHALL BE WELL AND ALL SHALL BE WELL
AND ALL MANNER OF THING SHALL BE WELL.

Song: How can I keep from singing?, CG 51, CH4 565; or Through the love of God,
our Saviour, CG 131, CH4 562

Blessing

May the God who holds us tenderly in the palm of Her/His hand, comfort us.
May the God who feeds us tenderly, direct us.
May the God who loves us tenderly, bless us,
Creator, Redeemer and Sustainer. Amen

Recessional song:

All is well

All is well,
this I know;
it is always safe
for me to change and grow.

Zam Walker

A PLACE OF REFUGE

A liturgy to celebrate the feast day of St Melangell, 27th May

Gathering

Come all who need rest.
COME TO THIS PLACE OF REFUGE.

Come all who need healing.
COME TO THIS PLACE OF WHOLENESS.

Come all who need challenge.
COME TO THIS PLACE OF ENCOURAGEMENT.

Come all called to be friends of God.
COME TO THIS PLACE OF WORSHIP.

Song: Lord, you have come, CG (*Common Ground*) 79; or Here I am, Lord, CG 50, CH4 (*Church Hymnary 4*) 251

Telling the story

Melangell (pronounced *M'langeth*) was an early British saint who lived in the seventh century. Having become a Christian, she fled from a forced marriage in Ireland to live an independent life devoted to prayer. She came to the Berwyn Mountains in Powys, Wales and settled in a secluded valley at a place called Pennant. She died in old age and her original grave slab still lies in the apse of the church there. The church has a circular ditch surrounding it and an ancient yew grove, which indicate that the site was sacred before Christianity. Melangell's shrine has been rebuilt in recent years and there is a healing centre attached to the church.

The legend of St Melangell comes from a medieval *Lives of the Saints*. One day a prince named Brochwell was hunting in the Berwyn Mountains. His hounds raised a hare which took refuge in a thicket. On pursuit, the prince found a young woman praying in the thicket, with the hare hiding under the folds of her garment. The hounds were urged on but fled away howling. The huntsman raised his horn to his lips but was unable to remove it. The young woman remained steadfast. She informed the prince that she dwelt at this place, and that she had fled there for refuge. The prince was so impressed by Melangell's holiness that he granted the valley to her; here Melangell founded a religious community for women. The prince also decreed that there would be no more hunting in the valley. To this day hares there are called 'Melangell's lambs'.

Meditation

What does refuge mean? A place of safety, shelter, security? Somewhere to run away to? Somewhere to be healed, to gather strength to go forward? Melangell resisted, by non-violent means, the violence of the forced marriage – the violence of other people's choices imposed upon her – and the violence against God's creation. She took action, risking her life, and remained true to her vision of how things should be. Action for justice and peace is integral to the gospel, not an optional extra. The Church should be a refuge in every sense: a place of sanctuary and healing, a shelter and a centre for re-energising.

Where do you find refuge? ...

Bible reading with prayer and response

Voice 1:   God is our refuge and our strength,
              a very present help in trouble. (Psalm 46)

Voice 2:   We pray for all in trouble,
              all who need sanctuary,
              all who need refuge from persecution and abuse.
              (Space to name situations and individuals)

ALL: Sung response: 'Stand firm' (Cameroon traditional, *There is One Among Us*, Wild Goose Publications)

Voice 1:   God is our refuge and our strength.
              Therefore we will not fear,
              though the earth should change,
              though the mountains shake in the heart of the sea,
              though its waters roar and foam,
              though the mountains tremble.

Voice 2:   We pray for all who are suffering due to environmental disaster,
              all who are homeless and destitute,
              all who need refuge from the forces of nature.
              (Space to name situations and individuals)

ALL: 'STAND, O STAND FIRM ...'

Voice 1:   God is our refuge and our strength.
              God makes wars cease;
              God breaks the bow and shatters the spear.

Voice 2:   We pray for all who live with war,

all who daily live in fear,
all who need refuge from violence.
(*Space to name situations and individuals.*)

ALL: 'STAND, O STAND FIRM ...'

Voice 1:   God is our refuge and our strength.
God says, 'Be still and know that I am God!'

Voice 2:   We pray for all who have no peace,
all who are anxious,
all who are too rushed,
all who need refuge from noise and busyness.
(*Space to name situations and individuals*)

ALL: 'STAND, O STAND FIRM ...'

Voice 1:   God is our refuge and our strength.
Jesus says, 'Come to me for rest
and I will bear your burden.'

Voice 2:   Jesus says, 'Come to me
and I will give you living water.
I will refresh and renew.'

ALL: GOD IS OUR REFUGE AND OUR STRENGTH.

Song: Mallaig sprinkling song, CG 82, CH4 722; or I heard the voice of Jesus say, CH4 540; or Be still and know that I am God CH4 754 or 755

Act of commitment (anointing hands)

Prayer

Living, loving God,
we come for refuge,
for peace, for renewal, for living water.

We bring our hands as a sign of our commitment
to work for justice and peace –
to create places of refuge.
We bring our hands
in the service of your kindom.*

Anointing of hands

During the anointing of hands the following chant could be sung:

Hands that loved

Words and music: David Coleman

Hands that loved and shaped the Earth;   us-ing ev-'ry hand here, bring new birth.

Affirmation

WE BELIEVE IN GOD WHO HAS CREATED
AND WHO IS CREATING,
WHO HAS DREAMED ALL THAT IS INTO BEING,
WHO IS THE HEARTBEAT OF CREATION.

WE BELIEVE IN GOD THE TRINITY,
TOGETHER THE MAKER, REDEEMER, SUSTAINER,
WHO CONSTANTLY SHOWS US THE WAY
TO BECOME WHO WE WERE CREATED TO BE.
WHO IS PERFECT COMMUNITY
AND THE ROOT OF ALL THAT IS.
WHO IS OUR REFUGE, OUR JOY AND OUR STRENGTH.

WE BELIEVE IN GOD WHO VALUES US
AND CHALLENGES US TO BRING THE WORLD INTO INCLUSIVE COMMUNITY,
WHO BRINGS JUSTICE AND CALLS US TO FRIENDSHIP.

WE BELIEVE IN THE KINDOM OF GOD:
THAT WE AND ALL CREATION ARE GOD'S FAMILY
AND ARE INTERDEPENDENT.

EACH PART IS NECESSARY TO THE WHOLE.
IF ONE PART SUFFERS OR IS SHUT OUT
THE KINDOM IS NOT FULLY REALISED.

WE BELIEVE THAT IN THE FACE OF GOD'S LOVE
OUR CALL IS TO FACE THE TRUTH AND NOT LIVE A LIE,
TO LIVE AUTHENTICALLY:

TO ACCEPT OURSELVES
AND TO FULFIL OUR POTENTIAL,
ENABLING OTHERS TO DO THE SAME.

WE ARE CALLED TO ABUNDANT LIFE,
ALWAYS GOING FORWARD NEVER HARKING BACK.
FOR GOD NEVER RESTORES
BUT ALWAYS MAKES NEW.

Song: Any lively, Pentecost song

Blessing

May God, the holy Trinity,
be a refuge for us and others,
and strengthen us to walk the way of justice and truth,
accompanying us into the unknown.
AMEN

Song: We will walk with God (Sizohamba naye), CH4 803; or The peace of the earth
be with you (CH4 798, CG 121)

Zam Walker

*Kindom – 'a word issuing from Mujerista theology [which] means that we are all kith and kin,
brothers and sisters in the new creation.' Mary Grey,* Introducing Feminist Images of God,
Sheffield Academic Press, 2001, p.117.

GARY

'People ask me how I can always be so happy,' says Gary, and tells me his story. About
how drug addicts broke into his flat and stole of his television and music system. Stabbed
him in the head and ribs thirteen times.

'I thought I was falling asleep, but I was really dying.'

'During it I had this feeling,' he says. 'Like someone suddenly reached out and
touched me. My guardian angel, my mum said. And I knew I was safe and held in love.'
Sunlight falls on Gary's face and he closes his eyes; he says the stabbing helped to clear
away the fog.

'People ask me how I can always be so happy – I'm back from death.'

He looks like he's on permanent vacation – standing in flowery, knee-length shorts, leather sandals, and a T-shirt proclaiming 'LIFE'S A BEACH'; a great smile across his broad, tanned face.

We're standing in the middle of the city sidewalk. People rush across to important meetings; wait with a clouded looks. Gary's bopping and dancing away.

I remind him about the last time I saw him. Down at the drop-in centre: pale and shivering in a corner, hugging himself.

'I wasn't pretty picture, eh?'

Gary tells me he moved and hardly goes there now, except to visit his friends. He likes to go on long walks – round Gilmour Park, the market, the botanical gardens … He's got energy to burn, energy he never knew he had.

'Here, look,' he says, and shows me the camera his father sent him, turns it over in his knuckly hands like treasure. 'I used to hate people taking *my* picture,' he laughs. 'I used to think I was ugly. Ugly inside and out, you know? Now I wear my shorts, take my shirt off. Why not?' he says, and shows me his zoom lens, 'there's nothing to be ashamed of.'

He doesn't care if people see his scars, or think he's crazy or stupid.

'God thinks I'm beautiful. Jesus calls me his beloved,' he says, standing openly – like he has stood in front of God's gaze and grown bright with it. Like something brilliant has happened, and he'll never feel ashamed again.

I ask him what he likes to take pictures of, and he says people he loves, things he loves. 'Sunsets and sunrises. Squares and fountains. Faces and flowers … I used to sit and watch TV. Now I wanna take pictures.'

Gary says he loves the way the light changes and is everywhere. 'So much I never even noticed before. You know?

'So that's why I listen to jazz,' he says, and shows me his Walkman now, fumbling excitedly. 'I used to listen to basement music – Black Sabbath, Iron Maiden. Now I listen to jazz. Walk around everywhere and take pictures and listen to jazz. I used to hate it. I didn't understand. The joy. The joy – but sadness too. Jazz people went through a lot, suffered. But it's the joy that comes through stronger in the end – Louis Armstrong, Ella Fitzgerald. I listen to the words. I never did before. They sink in. I used to hate it. I used to hate everything … Life was a bitch,' says Gary … 'I was sour, sittin' in a basement. I didn't understand.'

Gary shrugs. 'Sometimes you gotta die to be born,' he says, and starts showing me the photographs he keeps in his rucksack with a bottle of water; drops one the Spirit catches and carries off. 'Oh well, someone'll find it,' he says as it wings away.

Gary says he was dead. Dead when they climbed in his casket and stole his buried treasure. Now his treasure is the light that glitters. Each new day. 'I just thank God … See, listen,' he says, and reaches up and lays his hands on me: gives me his headphones.

'Can you hear? … See, light and dark. Sorrow and joy. Can you hear?' he trumpets. People passing glance around, wondering if he's talking to them. I listen. And can hear: the bluesy key, the brassy joy. I nod. He smiles widely.

While I'm standing listening to the music of life, Gary stands out on the street corner handing out photographs: waxy, shiny leaves of grass breaking up through the cement; blazing heads of flowers in the ruined shell of a building; the radiant dome of sky arching over apartment blocks and office towers … Gives one to a woman who stops, suddenly surprised … then smiles as something slowly sinks in. Hands one to a man who lights up and laughs. He seems to know who to give them to: people stopped or slowed with care and worry; people in a hurry who only have time for a bite. He seems to know: who needs energy, who needs some hope. I close my eyes – and can see pictures in the music …

I hand him back his halo.

Gary says when he walks through the mean street valley now he feels protected. 'Not wrapped in fog, tangled in sweat.' He smiles – the lines and wrinkles around his eyes all crinkly, radiating out. He looks lit up from within, his face beaming, his Hawaiian shorts like stained glass glowing.

The sun's come out and the world is full of light. It seems to me that Gary is making it that way – and he is. We shake hands like brothers and he strolls off, listening to the sea of life.

I watch him disappear down the street, taking pictures of everything in the world he nearly lost.

Heading uptown everything is lit up from within. The crucified, leafy trees; the lined faces of souls … Like a saint has passed this way trailing and spreading light. Like the fog has cleared.

There's a smell of tar rising in a heat haze; dazzle and glitter of sand dunes on a building site. There's a soft breeze; a warm, embracing feeling – I can feel the sun, sinking into my bones and heart. I want to run home and put my shorts on.

So, why are you so happy? people passing seem to ask.

I'm back from death.

Neil Paynter

VOYAGE – PENTECOST, 563 AD

(In 563 AD, St Columba journeyed from Ireland to the isle of Iona)

From rock and hearth to sea and sail,
from what we know and love
to what we've yet to know and yet to love,
You lead us, O Spirit of God.

As the wind in the sail,
as the breeze on our backs,
as the gale in all its force,
You drive us, O Spirit of God.

As the sea bears the barque,
borne along on the flowing tide,
thrown about by stormy wave,
so You carry us, O Spirit of God.

From sea and sail to our journey's end,
to rock and shore,
to haven and heaven,
You bring us, O Spirit of God.

And as a fire is lit in the hearth of the home,
so burn in the hearth of our heart,
and bless us, O Spirit of God.
Well bless us, O Spirit of God.

David Hamflett

THE PILGRIM ROAD

after St Columba

Words: Leith Fisher
Music: Timothy Redman
Arrangement: Sandy Small

2. Once more I dare the pilgrim road;
   the journey beckons on.
   I do not know what lies ahead –
   before the way is done
   make smooth the path beneath my feet
   until in you I stand complete.

3. And when the road seems hard and rough
   and perils loom ahead
   as faith grows dim while courage fails
   and hope's frail flame lies dead,
   come, kindly shepherd, cheer my way,
   and lead me through the darkest day.

4. So may it be that, as I go
   to travel day by day
   and faithful follow after you,
   the true and living way,
   your flame will warm, your star will guide,
   with your strong presence at my side.

LISTEN TO THEIR SILENCE

Listen to the sound of
silent women.
Unknown saints;
untold stories,
barely an imprint
of their passing.

Yet woven in the fabric
of creation,
hints and glimpses,
whispered shadows,
of lives as faithful,
true and Christ-like.

When you hear the songs of
Celtic brothers,
hear in the pauses
sounds of sisters,
who inspired, loved,
healed lifelong.

Chris Polhill

BRENDAN

Brendan the Voyager,
I salute you.

I delight in the stories of your travels:
of your lighting a bonfire
on the back of a whale,
of your readiness
to venture the unknown.

You make me ask myself
about the risks
I am willing to take
on my own journey.
You challenge my predilection
to curl up safe
in the warm.

Jesus, the Way,
make me more like Brendan:
ready to take risks
on my journey home.

Ruth Burgess

THEIR EARTHLY JOURNEY CLOSED

Words: Ian M. Fraser
Music: Donald Rennie

1. Their earth-ly jour-ney closed – not ma-ny well - re - nowned – their se - cret name dis - closed, life - sto - ries capped and crowned, rank up - on rank of com - mon folk hear Christ's: 'Well done! You bore my yoke!'

2. Some now in God rejoice,
   surprised he treats them so,
   who did not know that voice
   which called on them to go
   the sick to heal, the hungry feed,
   respond to every human need.

3. In God all thrill to find
   what neither eye nor ear
   nor human heart opined –
   prepared for those held dear –
   and what outstrips their utmost prayer:
   that God's own nature they should share.

4. Shall we discouraged be
   in fights for truth and peace
   who in such company
   the will of God embrace?
   For life is under God's control:
   in death his loved ones are made whole.

BEDE

Bede:
thinker
writer
biographer
monk.

Without you
our knowledge
would be smaller,
less full of facts and wonder.

You never travelled
beyond Wearmouth and Jarrow,
but you listened and learnt
from those who had.

You understood moons and tides;
you built up a library;
you had opinions about the dating of Easter;
you recorded the stories of soldiers and saints and kings;
you knew who was who,
and what was what,
in your own lands and beyond.

Your stories were glorious –
full of bright pictures,
dancing winter fires.
You told of the fragility and beauty of life
in an ounce of feathers and bones.*

We walk deep in your footsteps;
Bede the Venerable,
Bede the scientist,
Bede the friend of God.

Ruth Burgess

Bede told a story about a sparrow in wintertime to illustrate the fragility of life.

TRINITY

OPENING AND CLOSING RESPONSES FOR TRINITY SUNDAY

Cycle A

Ex 34:4–6, 8–9; Dan 3:52–56; 2 Cor 13:11–13; Jn 3:16–18

What is God like?
GOD IS CARING AND TENDER

What is God like?
GOD IS SLOW TO ANGER

What is God like?
GOD IS RICH IN KINDNESS

Maker, Jesus and Holy Spirit
GOD WELCOMES US WITH LOVE

> Be strong and happy
> Help one another
> WE WILL WALK TOGETHER IN JOY

> Work with each other
> Live in peace and justice
> WE WILL WALK TOGETHER IN HOPE

> Try to grow perfect
> Bless one another
> WE WILL WALK TOGETHER IN LOVE

Cycle B

Deut 4:32–34, 39–40; Ps 33; Rom 8:14–17; Mt 28:16–20

In the beginning, God the Maker:
JUST AND CREATIVE, STRONG AND LOVING

In the beginning, God the Storyteller:
JOYFUL AND HONEST, VULNERABLE AND QUESTIONING

In the beginning, God the Holy Spirit:
WISE AND GLORIOUS, WILD AND CHALLENGING

Alpha and Omega and now in this moment:
BLESSED BE THE TRINITY, BLESSED BE GOD

In us God lives
AND WE ARE HOLY

In us God cries
AND WE ARE HOLY

In us God loves
AND WE ARE HOLY

Baptised* and commissioned
WE GO OUT WITH JOY

'Baptised' could be substituted by 'blessed' where appropriate.

Cycle C

Prov 8:22–31; Ps 8; Rom 5:1–5; Jn 16:12–15

God the Maker
God of play and beauty
YOU LOVE US AND DELIGHT IN US

God the lover
God of tears and laughter
YOU LOVE US AND DELIGHT IN US

God the truth-teller
God of hope and adventure
YOU LOVE US AND DELIGHT IN US

When I see the heavens,
the work of your hands,
EVERYTHING INSIDE ME
WANTS TO JUMP FOR JOY!

By love and through the Maker
WE WILL WALK IN WONDER

By faith and through Jesus
WE WILL WALK IN JUSTICE

By hope and through the Holy Spirit
WE WILL WALK IN WISDOM AND IN JOY

Ruth Burgess

A PRAYER FOR TRINITY SUNDAY

In the mystery
of the beginning of things,
Creator God,
you made this planet,
rock upon layer of rock,
to be weathered and planted,
to become a place for living.

In the mystery
of human life,
Parent God,
you made us,
flesh and blood and spirit and bone,
image of yourself,
woman, man and child,
for loving.

In the mystery
of your unconditional love,
Redeemer God,
you came in Jesus,
flesh of our flesh, bone of our bone,
to buy us back from our captivity,
back to our true belonging, together,
daughters and sons of heaven,
living and loving
here on Earth.

So here, in this sacred place,
place of celebration,
of struggle, and of safety,
we rest,
content or cautious,
to know your presence,
hear your Word,
sense your Spirit,
welcoming us, and waiting,
once again.

And if, in the quiet,
there come to mind
the broken or the wounded bits
of our lives,
and of our world,
help us to name some of them now;
and as you have shared
our deepest sufferings,
so may the glue of your transforming grace
be for us,
and for our world,
a mending once again.

And if, in this place,
and at this table,
it will come to pass once again,
or perhaps for the very first time,
that your Spirit will touch ours –
then in your mercy
turn us to face you,
in ourselves, our world, our neighbour,
and send us out from here,
your companions on the way.

We pray in Jesus's name.

John Harvey

AUDACIOUSLY AND GRACIOUSLY

Words and melody: Ian M. Fraser
Arrangement: Duncan Anderson

1. Au - da - cious - ly and gra - cious - ly our hu - man frame's de - signed___ for rest and for ac - ti - vi - ty, in beau - ty and sim - pli - ci - ty, for la - bour and for ec - sta - sy – in liv - ing in - ter - twined___ through bod - ies we com - mu - ni - cate, our com - mon life to ce - le - brate.___

2. For caringly and daringly
   our sexual estate –
   in richness and diversity,
   in happy song and dance's sway,

in light of eyes and constancy,
in love – you did create,
who are the Father, Spirit, Son,
so manifold in life, yet one.

3. Delightedly, excitedly
   may we receive the gift,
   with thoughtfulness employing it
   and thrillingly enjoying it,
   preserved by grace from spoiling it:
   till human life we lift
   to join the feast, the dance, the fun
   which marks your life, great Three-in-One.

WITHOUT YOU

Without you,
Weaver of willows,
Spinner of sunrises,
I would have no place
to put my foot:
stumbling face first
into the mud puddles
of my mistakes.

Without you,
Retriever of the fallen,
Mediator of the sin-splattered,
I would have no place
to put my soul:
adrift on the stormy sea
of seduction,
at the mercy of
bedlam's blows.

Without you,
Whisperer of wisdom,
Gift-bearing dove,
I would have no place
to put my heart:

watching it shrivel
in despair's
bitter grasp.

In you
I find my place,
Father, Son and Holy Spirit:
Blessed Trinity,
in you.

Amen

Thom M. Shuman

TRANSFORMATION

I need your touch
O my Creator!

The Father's touch of healing:
pain released
brokenness remade
the marred image restored.

The Son's touch of love:
frozenness melted
loneliness assuaged
tears turned to laughter.

The Spirit's touch of liberation:
freedom from the past
power for the present
courage for the future.

Touch me
O my Creator
that I may be transformed!

Pat Bennett

ALPHA, OMEGA AND EMMANUEL
IN THE INNER CITY

Alpha – beginnings

In the beginning, God created man.
But God said, 'It is not good for him to be alone.'
So he created woman;
and they became a family,
and families lived together,
and formed communities
and cities.

In the city there are constant new beginnings:
dawn breaking over the harsh grey tower blocks;
sunlight flooding the flats;
the hustle and bustle of children shouting on their way to school;
the awakening multicultural buzz;
the clashing of energies as residents struggle against injustice – marginalisation,
victimisation, media-crucifixion ...
the difficult working through of differences;
the rebuilding after setbacks, destruction (cars being burned), riots;
the birth pangs of something better coming into being from the people.

God is there in the painful beginnings:
in the cry of the unplanned for, unwanted child;
in the despair of yet another day of unemployment;
in another day of working in a sweatshop for an unfair wage;
in the start of another long lonely day for the housebound.

Omega – endings

The sun sets over the city,
its colours glorious,
before the darkness enfolds a million homes,
the homecomings and welcomes,
quiet talking and sharing of evening meals,
with family,
with friends of different cultures.
Lights shining into the darkness from a million windows;
rest and sleep for weary workers.

God is there too in the dark endings:
for abused children in nightly fear of the return of drunken parents;
for children and young people wandering the streets late into the night –
no one caring enough to call them home;
for those for whom darkness is a cover for their wrongdoing;
for homeless people bedding down in shop doorways.

Emmanuel – God-with-us

The With-us-God:
in hidden acts of kindness amongst neighbours;
in bridges built, and strangers trusted;
in the building of a new health centre,
or a garden,
or a playground –
in the building of community in a fragmented world;
in refugees and asylum-seekers being welcomed –
in diversity being honoured and enjoyed;
in the recognising of the image of God in one another.

But also with us in times of selfishness and power-struggles,
in relationships broken and community destroyed,
in exclusiveness and bigotry.
God-with-us wanting to challenge, redirect and empower.

In what way can God be the Beginning, the Ending and the With-us-God for everyone?
For those with hope and vision for the future,
and for those for whom each day brings dread and despair –
rejoicing with those building relationships and community,
weeping over the power-struggles and divisions?

God has no ears and eyes but mine,
no voice but mine,
no body language but mine,
no hands but mine.

The Lord said to Isaiah:
'Whom shall I send, and who will go for us?'

'Here I am, send me.'

Frances Hawkey

THE TRINITY AS A CIRCLE

We set a puzzle in Christianity by saying there is only one God and then talking of three – Father, Son and Holy Spirit. We say this is a mystery: three persons but one God. Three sides, like the three leaves of the clover leaf; three 'states', like water, mist and ice, but one element – but still most Christians feel confused about the Trinity. We need to understand as much as we can or we lose a great gift.

The most common misunderstanding is to think of the Trinity as an isosceles triangle, with the Father on top, and Jesus and the Holy Spirit referred to by name but definitely not coequal with Him. Here we project onto God our own hierarchical way of ordering life – very effective for good management, business and industry, and makes for an efficient army, but not healthy or helpful when we talk about God. This model is often what we say and do, but it is not in our beliefs; no theologian would agree with this view of one major and two lesser persons of the Trinity. We need to repent and be sorry of how we live with this view; there is no hierarchy within God.

The traditional model that is reflected in old churches does not help either, as it too suggests a hierarchy within God: the line of the building – with the Holy Spirit in the nave, Jesus at the sanctuary steps, and the Father at the altar. In the past, a screen (with the image of the crucified Jesus at the top, often Mary, his mother, and John on either side, and people rising out of graves at the bottom) separated the nave and sanctuary: Pray in the power of the Spirit, through Jesus to the Father. It is a neat way of solving the puzzle – and plenty of theologians are happy with it; so if you like it and find it helpful, fine. I find it unacceptable: it is hierarchy in another form. We need the combined power of Jesus and the Holy Spirit to approach the Father. This model leaves the Father very remote; distances us from our Creator. So for me it won't do.

Another thing we tend to do is to believe in the coequal relationship, so we see the Trinity as an equilateral triangle, but then only talk to one point, one person of the Trinity. Typically, but not universally, 'traditional' Christians address God as Father, evangelicals talk to Jesus, and charismatics speak to the Holy Spirit. By doing this we miss out on the liberation of the Trinity, and so fail to live out the difference it makes to our relationship with God and with each other.

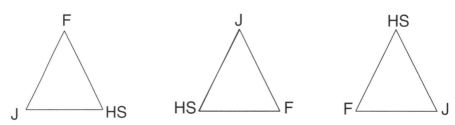

But if we see the Trinity as a circle – no beginning or ending, no top or bottom, God an existing and eternal relationship – Jesus can say: 'I am in the Father and the Father is in me.' This is the relationship we are invited to join, so that we pray *in* God and not *to* God. Here we see God committed to the dance of an equal and unending relationship, willing to suffer rather than force us into relationship. We see the Father and the Holy Spirit in agony with Jesus on the Cross, so close is the relationship – in Greek icons you always see some representation of each person of the Trinity on the Cross. We are invited to be in this relationship, part of the dance, knowing 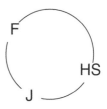 the vulnerability and the joy of love. Instead of constantly searching for the way to God, whenever we pray we dwell *in* God, in the Living God – Father, Son and Holy Spirit – our Creator, Redeemer, Sustainer.

Chris Polhill

KNOWING HER BLESSING

Loving Mother,
who with perfect timing
knows when to push; to nudge; to shove;
and when to wait,
even though panting for change.
Grant us the courage to name you;
and the grace of your timing.

Sister Christ,
who feeds us with warm breast milk
when the heavenly feast is too rich a fare;
and in whose death our own wounds find resurrection.
Teach us also to play with you,
that we may know the delight
of your particular freedom.

Lady Wisdom,
who nurtures and wills our growing.
Lead us in your wild dance,
that we may tread the unfamiliar paths
singing gladly;
and find fulfilment for the dreams
that fit your knowing of us.

Chris Polhill

WAYFARING

God be the road on which you travel:
He the mountains
on which you are tested and challenged
He the wells
at which you find healing and peace.

Christ be the light by which you travel:
He the vision
which informs and enlarges you
He the lodestar
shining in your darkest nights.

The Spirit inspire you as you travel:
She the restlessness
driving you onwards
She the stillness
leading you to the heart of God.

The Trinity, the Three,
go with you as you travel;
and may your journey
begin
continue
and end
in Them

Pat Bennett

ENVIRONMENTAL DAYS

BE NICE TO NETTLES WEEK

Be Nice to Nettles Week was set up in 1991 by the Cramlington Organisation for Nature and the Environment (CONE). See www.nettles.org.uk and www.workingwithwildlife.co.uk

THE DOCKEN LEAF OF YOUR LOVE

God of the sharp, stinging nettle,
and the soft, furry, white, dead nettle,
we praise you for our senses
which help us to enjoy the world around us.

Thank you for the tangy taste of nettle soup,
and for Northumbrian nettle cheese;
for the tender touch of dead nettle leaves
brushing against bare skin.

Help us to be sensitive to others:
When we are nettled by their actions
or stung by a harsh retort,
may we respond with gentle words,

healing hurts with the docken leaf of your love,
known and experienced through Jesus,
who noticed the flowers of the field
and the seed that fell in the nettlebed,

and who taught us to recognise
that we are all God's children,
created to delight in the diversity of the earth –
from the towering grandeur of tall trees,
to the humble, unpretentiousness of nettles.

Carol Dixon

PICKING NETTLES

Use protection when picking nettles: wear heavy-duty gloves or gauntlets, thick trousers and waders or wellingtons.

Stings: If you can't find a docken leaf to rub on the affected area, try an aromatic herb such as mint or rosemary.

Elizabeth Paterson

NETTLE SOUP

Ingredients:

1 litre of stock (chicken or vegetable)
8–10 handfuls of nettles (Wearing protective gloves, pick only the tops and young leaves.)
1 medium onion
Oil and seasoning
Flour for thickening

Preparation:

Wearing kitchen gloves, wash the nettles well and discard any thick stalks.
Chop the onion.
Heat the oil and sauté the onion till soft.
Add the nettles and stir till well mixed.
Add the stock and seasoning.
Bring to the boil and simmer gently for five minutes.
Liquidise or pass through a sieve.
Mix about a dessert spoon of flour and a small amount of water into a smooth paste.
Add the flour paste to the soup.
Reheat the soup, stirring until it thickens.
Check seasoning
Serve in a bowl with a swirl of cream or plain yoghurt.

Elizabeth Paterson

NETTLE SOUP

Ingredients:

A large pan full of nettle tops, i.e. the top few young leaves when first growing in spring, and as little stalk as possible. (Collect wearing gloves and well away from roads.)
1 onion
1 clove garlic
500g carrots
1 tbsp oil
Herb mix and grated ginger, or stock cube
1 pint water or stock
Salt and pepper to taste

Exact proportions of the ingredients is not important: suit your own taste – more onion gives a stronger taste, more carrot a sweeter taste.

Preparation:

In a soup pot, sauté chopped onion and crushed garlic in the oil on a low heat. When soft, add herb mix/ginger and water. Or, if not using herb mix, add water or stock and stock cube. Add sliced carrots, salt and pepper, and bring to a boil.

Wearing kitchen gloves, strip away any stalk and thoroughly wash the nettle tops in a colander; shake off excess water. Add the nettles to the soup; boil then simmer. The sting goes as soon as the nettles are in boiling water.

Blend or sieve the soup.

Serve.

Chris Polhill

NETTLE TEA

Nettle tea is thought to be good for people with anaemia or arthritis. (Check with your doctor before drinking nettle tea.)

Loosely fill a litre jug with young nettle leaves; pour in boiling water to cover. Leave standing 2–3 minutes, strain and drink either hot or cold. A little lemon juice may be added to improve the flavour.

Elizabeth Paterson

NETTLES GROWING IN THE GARDEN

Nettles add a high amount of nitrogen to the soil and so stimulate the growth of other plants – it is very useful to have them planted near soft fruits.

Elizabeth Paterson

COMPOST

Freshly cut nettles added to the compost heap raise the temperature of the compost, encouraging the decomposition of vegetable matter.

Elizabeth Paterson

TO DETER MILDEW, BLACKFLIES AND APHIDS ON PLANTS

Wearing protective gloves, put all parts of the nettle plant into a container and press down lightly; cover with water (rain water is best). Leave 7–14 days – the longer you leave it the stronger the solution will be. Strain, and dilute with water (a ratio of 1:1 if you left it standing for 7 days; a ratio of 3:1 if you left it standing for 14 days). Add a small amount of liquid soap to help the mixture adhere to the plant leaves. Spray affected plants as required.

Elizabeth Paterson

A PRAYER FOR WORLD OCEAN DAY

Living God,
Creator of the bright blue sea
and each grain of sand,
of the minuscule plankton
and the majestic whale,
forgive us for pillaging the seas of our planet,
polluting them with oceans of waste
that destroy the fragile ecosystems of our earth.

Help us to work with you
to restore the balance of nature –
to care for your creation today,
so that people of tomorrow can share
the rich heritage you have given us.

Carol Dixon

RECYCLING – RESOURCES FOR A SERVICE OF COMMITMENT

The following piece was taken from a service of commitment held in Iona Abbey in 2005. It can be adapted to a local context.

Introduction

Leader: Humans created a wonderful new material. It was extremely versatile and could be tailored to meet very specific technical needs. It was lighter in weight than competing materials. It was extremely durable. It was resistant to water, impact and certain chemicals. It had good safety and hygiene properties for food packaging. It had excellent thermal and electrical insulation properties. Last but not least, it was relatively inexpensive to produce. The humans called this wonderful new material: plastic. Evening passed and morning came – the umpteenth day.

We love plastic so much that the world's annual consumption of plastic materials is now nearly 100 million tonnes. Nearly 3 million tonnes of plastic material is produced in the UK every week. What you see lying around the Abbey here tonight is just some of the plastic used here in the last two weeks.

Many of us now recycle and facilities are increasing. However, the most recent survey reports that only 5.5% of all plastic bottles sold in the UK is collected for recycling.

Not everyone is called to environmental campaigning. We can't all do everything. But we are all called to be responsible for the consequences of our actions. To come to a beautiful island and to commit, or recommit, ourselves to following Jesus (while allowing our lifestyles to threaten God's creation) would be hypocritical. So if you choose to commit yourself to Jesus tonight, please also commit yourself to doing one more thing towards caring for the environment. Perhaps you already do a lot. Even the 'smallest' action makes a difference: recycling, reusing, reducing, driving less and in a more fuel efficient way, saving up to install solar panels, the list is never-ending ...

As a symbol of your commitment, please leave your seat and take a plastic bottle from the crossing, or the font, or the chancel; many of you have taken beach stones from Iona over the years. These bottles weigh a fraction of those stones and can be squashed flat. When you get home, put your bottle in your local recycling facility, or recycle the bottle but keep the bottle top, as a reminder of your commitment to God's creation. If you are not leaving the island in the next few days, you could put your bottle in the recycling bins in the centres here.

Listen first to a prayer from the United Nations Environmental Sabbath Programme:

Great Spirit,
give us hearts to understand
never to take from creation's beauty more than we can give,
never to destroy wantonly for the furtherance of greed,
never to deny to give our hands for the building of earth's beauty,
never to take from her what we cannot use.

Give us hearts to understand that to destroy earth's music is to create confusion,
that to wreck her appearance is to blind us to her beauty,
that to callously pollute her fragrance is to make a house of stench,
that as we care for her
she will care for us.
Amen

Liz Gibson

Statistics taken from Wastewatch www.wasteonline.org.uk

JOINING CHURCH

GETTING THE WEAN DONE

I believe in God the Father Almighty, Maker of heaven and earth …
from the Apostles' Creed

I well remember it was a summer's evening when this young lassie came in to see me in my office in the church in the Gallowgate.

I knew the girl a bit, but not too well. She was sixteen years old. For the purposes of this story we'll call her Mary.

After inviting her to sit down, I asked her what I could do for her. 'I want my wean★ done,' she said.

So we started to chat about her baby, who was just a few weeks old: me asking if it was a good baby, did it sleep at night?, and so on. You know the kind of thing. And she was obviously really proud of the baby, telling me that in every way she was a wee smasher.

Then I asked, 'Why do you want your baby done?' – a perfectly normal question for a minister to ask someone who was never around the church. Like most ministers, I was assuming that she had little real idea of what the Church understands baptism to be, and that she was probably coming because of some superstitious notion that christening was 'lucky', or something like that. (Oh, our arrogance!)

So I asked again, 'Why do you want your wean done?'

The girl looked at me stunned, as if she'd never heard such a stupid question before. 'What do you mean, *why do I want my wean done*? I just want it done, that's all!'

'Oh, I know you want it done,' I said, 'but *why* do you want it done?'

And this kind of daft conversation went on for a wee while with the girl getting more and more frustrated at this dunderheid★ behind his impressive desk; until eventually, standing up and putting her hands on my desk and leaning over until her nose was almost rammed into mine, she screamed at me, 'Do you no understand? God gives us the wean, doesn't he? So the wean has to be done!'

Suddenly, the minister, with all his expensive university education, realised that he was hearing, from a sixteen year old unmarried mother from Barrowfield, as clear a statement of belief in God the giver of life as he was ever going to hear.

Erik Cramb

★'Wean' is a commonly used Glasgow name for a baby or toddler.
★'Dunderheid' means thickhead – extremely dense!

IT HAPPENED AGAIN YESTERDAY

It happened again yesterday:

Jesus took two little children and put them among us during morning worship, and we saw the kingdom around us: Two sisters, one 10 and the other 6, were brought forward to be baptised. The words we speak at every baptism were spoken, the promises we make at every baptism were made, the Apostles' Creed was affirmed once again.

Then the prayer over the water was made – and the Spirit began to play in it, laughing and splashing with delight. She allowed me to caress the living waters and bring them to Caroline and Leigh Ann:

A palmful for the God of grace,
A palmful for the Christ of love,
A palmful for the Spirit of life.

And as I touched their heads, I saw the baptismal waters reflected in the tears brimming in the eyes of their parents.

And last night, when Leigh Ann and her mum were out in their backyard watering their vegetable garden, Leigh Ann (who has some developmental challenges) dipped her hand in the cool water, and then placed it on her mum's head three times, repeating the words spoken to her that morning.

No wonder Jesus tells us we have to become like children in order to enter the kingdom of heaven. They get it.

Thom M. Shuman

JESUS RISEN FROM THE GRAVE

(Tune: Leibster Jesu)

Jesus, risen from the grave,
we would greet you with thanksgiving.
Gloriously you came to save –
bring new life to all our living.
By your dying love's endeavour
we are yours both now and ever.

Cross and passion are entwined
in your resurrection glory;
may that vision claim our minds,
help us live out love's new story.
By your mighty Spirit's blowing
fill our lives to overflowing.

To receive this sign of grace,
these, our children, we now bring you.
Seal your love in their heart's place:
Praises may they ever sing you.
As they grow, your service learning;
all their days, for you their yearning.

Bound in love, by love made one,
serving, sharing, hoping, giving,
working out what love's begun
day by day in all our living.
Lord of costly love and glory,
in us form your deathless story.

Leith Fisher

SHOT THROUGH AND THROUGH WITH WONDER

Words and melody: Ian M. Fraser
Arrangement: Donald Rennie

1. Shot through and through with won - der___ this sa - cra - ment of grace! The Lov - er and be - lov - ed are here come face to face, and em - brace.

2. The water holds a promise,
   the promise bears a sign
   that lives once drowned with Jesus
   in his true love entwine
   – yours and mine.

3. We can live resurrection
   whatever tests our way,
   and love and live for others,
   and for God's Kingdom Day
   fight and pray.

4. We offer then our bodies,
   a living sacrifice,
   and reaffirm our baptism
   convinced – when this life dies
   it will rise.

HUNGRY AND THIRSTY FOR JUSTICE

It had been a long hot day of protest.
Church members were out in force
on the steps of the Pentagon.
It was the sixties.
The banners read 'Vietnam'.

Elizabeth, aged six,
was with her parents,
and was hungry
and thirsty.

'Mum, what's there to eat?'

The bread and wine of a requiem mass
were being passed around the crowd,
and provided the answer to Elizabeth's question.

How,
thought her mother,
do I explain to her lifelong-church-attending grandmother –
who is of the strong opinion that religion and politics
should never mix –
that her granddaughter's first communion
just happened.

Ruth Burgess

AN EASTER BLESSING

The class for new communicants had gathered with the minister for their first meeting, and in the small church vestry there was a sense of intimacy and expectation. The faces were familiar: regular worshippers, new attenders, and young people from church families.

All six communicants were women. Their ages varied, but they had all, in their own way and for their own purposes, responded to the invitation to come to learn, to make up the year's group of enquirers. Their journey of sharing and growing would take them to an Act of Commitment on Easter Sunday.

Because not everyone in the group knew each other, the minister began that first meeting with a simple question: 'Why have you come to join this class?' It seemed the obvious starting point, and would allow each person to say their piece; it would clarify everyone's needs for their journey of learning and establish the ground on which the group would travel.

Gently, the participants offered their reasons for coming. The replies were predictable: 'Brought up in the church …' 'Been through Sunday school and Bible class …' 'Getting married, and needing to think about what a church marriage is about …' 'Baby to be baptised, and thinking about deeper things …' 'Big sister joined the church last year …' All good stuff, and offered with sincerity; it was, for the minister, familiar and helpful territory.

One young lady was left to offer her response. She had listened intently to the others, and now it was her turn. The minister made it easy for her. 'Well, Linda – last but not least. Why have you come along?'

There was a pause … Then Linda smiled. With a gentle voice, she offered her story. 'When I was fourteen,' she began, 'my granny died. She was old and frail, and she had been ill for a while. She hadn't had much of a life since my grandpa died, so it was her time to go. It was the first death I had experienced, and it was all a bit unreal.'

She stopped, and took a deep breath. The room was still, and everyone was already deeply involved with Linda's story. Then she continued: 'I went to my granny's funeral. I didn't know whether I should or not, but I loved my granny so it was the right thing to do. I didn't know what to expect really, because I'd never been to a funeral before. And, to be honest, it was all pretty dull. The minister was nice, but he was old and –' The group glanced at the minister – far from old – then back at Linda, who was smiling widely. 'Well, he wasn't as modern as you!' she told the minister. Laughter all round …

'I don't remember much about the service, though he did say some nice things about granny. But when the service was over, something weird happened. The minister came to the front row where me and my mum and my brother were sitting, and he shook hands with each of us in turn. And, as he did so, he looked my mother and brother in the eye and he said: "God bless you." When he came to me, he did the same: "God bless you," looking right at me. And I looked straight back at him and said: "And God bless you too." I don't know why I said that. I don't really know what it means. But I've never been able to get that moment out of my mind.'

You could have heard a pin drop. No one moved. Linda started to cry gently. 'I don't know why "God bless you" has come to matter so much. I still don't know what it means. So I've decided it's time to find out … And that's why I'm here.'

There were nods. There were smiles of recognition. One of the other participants passed Linda a tissue. An older woman by her side took her hand.

'Aye, hen, you're right enough. I guess that's why we're all here. "God bless you" is for me too. We'll just have to find out what it means together.'

Linda's 'God bless you' became a mantra for the class. People would greet each other with these words when the class gathered. They would say goodbye with the same blessing. And it mapped out all the territory in between. Together the group learned what it meant for them.

In the special Easter service, 'God bless you' was very real to everyone present. As each new communicant knelt in their act of commitment, hands were laid on them, and 'God bless you' was said, and meant, and felt.

'God bless you' had made that Easter very special.

'God bless you' offered to a fourteen-year-old at a time of death, in an unfamiliar setting, in the dullness of worship – perhaps without much thought or self-belief – had started a journey of learning and growing that the young Linda could never have expected.

'God bless you' offered in response, even when it wasn't clear what the words meant, was a signpost on that day that pointed in a new direction.

Tom Gordon

BIG TOMMY'S CONFIRMATION

So there I was at the appointed time. The intimation on the previous Sunday had read: 'Anyone interested in an enquirers' class for first communicants should come to the vestry on Wednesday evening at 7:30 for the introductory meeting.' And in the vestry on the Wednesday evening I sat and waited.

It was 7:30. No one came. I looked at the copies of the *Good News Bible* I'd brought through from the church. No one came. I packed away the copies of *A Faith for the '70s* and *A Lenten Study Guide* – twelve copies of each on the vestry table – which I was going to use as background material for the class. No one came. I thought of the well-worn editions of *A Compact Concordance* and *One Volume Bible Commentary* I had in my briefcase. No one came.

It was 7:45. 'Why am always so optimistic,' I asked myself – I knew that similar classes on previous years had numbered one, none, none, two, and one.

I let out a heavy sigh as I put on my coat and picked up my keys.

There was a knock at the door. Puzzled, I pulled the door open and there stood Big Tommy, the last person I expected to see. Tommy was a well-known figure around the parish. He was from a local family, the oldest of eight boys, and, to be honest, Tommy was not at all bright. 'A couple of cans short of a six-pack' was one of the more gentle descriptions of this big, amiable man. Tommy was in his late twenties and had never worked; he dotted around the parish being nice to people and doing odd jobs. He had the reading age of a child and the body of a giant. His hands were like shovels.

Tommy came to church regularly. What he made of it all, I was never quite sure. He would come to the front for the children's talk and laugh and have fun with the little ones. No one minded. It was just Tommy. Sometimes he would fall asleep during the service. Occasionally he would wander out and then in again. Often he would make a strange wailing sound during the singing of the hymns. But no one minded. It was just Tommy.

I liked Tommy. Everyone did. And Tommy seemed to like everyone too.

'Tommy,' I asked, with an obvious air of incredulity, 'what brings you here? I was just about to put the lights out and go home.'

'Ah've come for the thing,' Tommy replied.

'The thing, Tommy, what thing?'

'What you said on Sunday about being here on Wednesday for …' Tommy was struggling for the words. '… The … class … you said … tonight … to come, you said … anyone … for first comic cants, you said … so I came … like you said … eh …'

By now the breathless Tommy was well into the vestry and was taking his coat off and making himself at home. I did likewise. It seemed the sensible thing to do. So Tommy and I sat across from each other, and Tommy patiently waited for the 'first comic cants' class to begin. I thought of *A Faith for the '70s* in the vestry cupboard. And I pondered Tommy's reading age. I remembered the concordance and commentary in my briefcase. And I reflected on Tommy's IQ. I wondered about the *Good News Bible* and the *Lenten Study Guide*. And I mused on the kind of books – or comics, indeed – Tommy would be familiar with.

I said the only thing I could think of saying: 'Why are you here, Tommy? Why did you come tonight?'

Tommy smiled. 'I like you,' he grinned. 'I like it in church. It's fun. You're funny, and you make me happy inside. People don't tell me to go away or look all nasty when I sing. I feel all tingly inside when I hear the stories you tell from the Bible. I like the one about the rolls and the fish. I like fish-fingers. Do you like them too? And I think it's funny when the Protestant son feeds pigs, and comes back to his dad, and his dad runs to meet him. My dad runs too, but only to catch the bus in the morning. And Jesus sounds fun too, eh? Jesus and the children. I like that. You like children too, eh? 'Cause they laugh when they're in church, eh, an' church is fun. D'you think Jesus would like me, eh? 'Cause that would be nice, eh? D'you think so, eh?'

Any idea I had of correcting Tommy's biblical interpretations – 'prodigal' for 'Protestant', and the like – didn't last long. All thoughts of study guides and Bibles and commentaries vanished in an instant, as I absorbed the significance of Tommy's breathless credo.

And that's the way it was for the six evenings Big Tommy and I spent together through Lent. We swapped stories. We talked about people who loved us. We laughed at Bible tales. We shared what it was like to be hugged. We told each other how much we liked one another. We talked secretly about some of the people in the parish. We compared notes on things we liked: fish-fingers, jogging dads and all. And we learned. Together we learned. We learned about each other. We learned about acceptance. We learned about being the Church. We learned about Jesus. We learned about real creeds. We learned about faith. We learned about being loved.

So that's why one new communicant stood before the congregation on Easter morning. One Tommy McAlister – resplendent in his good suit and grinning from ear to ear.

'Do you believe in one God, Father, Son and Holy Spirit, and do you confess Jesus Christ as your Saviour and Lord?' I should have asked. But instead, I asked, 'Is Jesus your friend, Tommy?'

'Aye,' was his bold reply.

'Do you feel at home in our church?' I asked.

'Aye, I like it here,' was his grinning reply.

'Tommy McAlister, God loves you today – as he's always loved you – and the church loves you too. You belong to Jesus and his Church. You are always welcome here.' And the words of an Easter confirmation were done.

The beaming Tommy gave me a huge bear hug after the service. I cried. I'd studied and learned at Big Tommy's feet, and felt as blessed by Tommy's embrace as he'd felt by being welcomed into the church again that Easter Day.

Tom Gordon

MAKING AND
KEEPING PROMISES

TWO ORDINATION PRAYERS

ORDINATION

Called first and foremost to follow Christ.
Grown in obscurity, in unlikely places.
Called again to lead Christ's people.
Called in weakness to walk in Christ's strength.
Called in emptiness to share Christ's fullness.
Called in poverty to share Christ's riches.
Called in darkness to share Christ's light.
Called in the ordinary to reflect Christ's beauty.
Called to serve Christ.
Strengthened, equipped, enriched and beautified.
Called by Christ alone.

TRUE BEAUTY

Lord Jesus Christ,
icon of the Father,
you are true beauty,
not in triumph at the right hand of the Father
but in your crucified nakedness.
In the vulnerability of the crucifixion
you are truly beautiful.

I, a woman,
icon of the Father.
My beauty found in Christ alone.
Not in the triumph of resurrection life,
but in my crucifixion with Christ.
In entering the vulnerability of Christ
is found my true beauty.

Lord, as my ordination draws on,
may beauty be found not in triumph,
music, ceremony,
but in the years to come,
in the vulnerability of service.

In years to come, Lord, may you see in me,
a woman, icon of the Father,
true beauty.
Icon of Christ.
Vulnerable, naked, there for all to see.

Anne Lawson

'True beauty' was written the day before Anne Lawson's ordination as a deacon. It grew out of ideas from a talk by Bishop John Finney.

THREE PRAYERS OF CONSECRATION

THIS YEAR'S JOURNEYING

Lord –
I consecrate myself to You
in this year's journeying:

Take my feet
from the safety of the shallows
out into the challenge
of unexplored depths.

Take my heart
from the sterility of selfish preoccupations
to the fruitfulness
of wounded love.

Take my mind
from the narrowness of human thought
to the expansiveness
of divine insight.

Take my hands
from the poverty of having and keeping
to the riches
of giving and sharing.

Take my voice
from the blandness of safe religion
to the proclamation
of Your radical Kingdom.

Lord –
I consecrate myself to You
in this year's journeying:

Take my life
from safety to risk
from coldness to love
from darkness to light
from selfishness to sharing
from silence to proclamation.

Take my life for Your Kingdom!

HERE IS MY LIFE

Lord – here are my feet
hesitant, stumbling.
Take them and lead them
from the safe, familiar pathways
out into the dark unknown.

Lord – here are my hands
weak, empty.
Take them and fill them
that they may be empowered and equipped
for the building of Your Kingdom.

Lord – here is my mind
rational, proud.
Take it and enlighten it
that my arrogant assumptions may yield
to a truer understanding of Your will and ways.

Lord – here is my heart
unbroken, guarded.
Take it and wound it
that I may never again be free
of Your pain for this suffering world.

Lord – here is my life
small, surrendered.
Take it and indwell it
that my whole being may resonate with Your love
and overflow with Your Life!

FOR THE LIFE OF YOUR WORLD

Lord of the journey – I offer You my feet;
take them and anoint them
that I might go out into the barren places
run towards the prodigal
travel the extra mile.

Lord of compassion – I offer You my hands;
take them and free them
that I might reach out to the rejected
tend the wounds of the broken
wash the feet of the poor.

Lord of the Gospel – I offer You my voice;
take it and strengthen it
that I might proclaim the reign of Your Kingdom
speak out against injustice
ask hard questions.

Lord of wisdom – I offer You my mind;
take it and enlighten it
that I might see with the eye of an eagle
uncover new possibilities
reach beyond the obvious.

Lord of love – I offer You my heart;
take it and wound it
that I might share in the pain of the suffering
become a home for the lost
love without calculation.

Lord of eternity – I offer You my life;
take it and spend it
for the life of Your world.

Pat Bennett

SEE, IT IS DONE

(Tune: Melita or Sussex Carol)

See, it is done; yet still not done:
Christ's work accomplished opens up
a journey which must be begun
that all creation may retrieve
that promised and abundant life
entrusted, if we but believe.

One thing is done – the sacrifice
where God spares not the only Son
who for us takes the rap, and dies
in agony and shame. Thus done,
to free creation, is that work,
the dying and the rising won.

Not done – the fight to conquer sin;
not done – the pilgrimage of faith;
not done – true ways which will begin
to give the poor their honoured place:
begun, not done, nor will be done
till God's reign sheds abroad its grace.

To put on Christ is to believe
it shall be done by a new birth:
for we are heirs who now receive
abundant life, where once was death:
for justice, truth and peace we'll strive,
empowered to heal this broken earth.

Ian M. Fraser

CHRIST!

Thank you for the baby Jesus,
though he sometimes doesn't please us.
Perhaps, dear God, a bit of curbing –
Jesus can be so disturbing.

Made the waves, calmed the water,
came to save, came to slaughter.
Came with love to banish fear,
disturbing all that we hold dear.

A banquet offered for your crust;
delusions crumbling into dust.
Light and mirror, fiery sword –
Christ can be disturbing, Lord.

Stuart Barrie

DEVOTED AS I AM

Devoted as I am
to the teachings of
my financial guru,
my political party,
my fitness trainer,

I pick and choose
from your Word –
disregarding it when
it makes me uncomfortable.

Devoted as I am
to accumulating
more and more stuff,

it is difficult
to entrust my junk
to those who would
consider it treasure.

Devoted as I am to
my securities,
my pension,
my future,

I find it easy
to pass by those
for whom each day
is such a struggle.

You have hallowed me
with your overflowing gifts,
O God:
help me to give
myself away to others
completely.
Amen

Thom M. Shuman

BEING CHURCH

GATHERING

Lord,
in this shared time
we offer ourselves
to each other.

We offer our understandings and insights –
not to dominate or overthrow one another
but that we ourselves
might be challenged and changed.

We offer our emotions and experiences –
not in self-indulgence
but that through honesty and openness
we may find and give encouragement and comfort.

We offer our skills and talents –
not because of pride in our abilities
but in a joyful recognition and sharing
of your overflowing bounty.

And as we celebrate and offer our common humanity,
the very flesh and fabric of our lives,
may you,
the Incarnate One,
be once again embodied here
in our individuality
and our community.

Pat Bennett

BEING CHURCH

My first parish church as a minister was 'The Old Kirk of Edinburgh'. 'The Old Kirk', now at the heart of a deprived housing estate, had its roots in St Giles' Cathedral, and had a history stretching back 300 years and more.

Much of church life at the Old Kirk was about trying to find meaning in the midst of chaos, faith in the midst of deprivation. The congregation was small, but the people were committed. They knew what it was to be a small light in a great darkness. And their light shone very brightly indeed.

Tradition mattered, as familiar things offered people some security in an ever-changing world. One such tradition, uncommon in the Church of Scotland, was the frequent celebration of the Sacrament of Holy Communion; in the Old Kirk this took place every second Sunday. The style of celebrating Communion was distinctive: people were invited to come and sit round tables at the front of the church – a style familiar to those who have shared an evening Communion in Iona Abbey. It used to be that way in many churches in Scotland, where the Communion table would be in the centre of worship.

One Sunday the church was prepared for Communion as usual; as the celebrant, I stood at the head of the table and invited people to come to share in the Sacrament. There were thirty places round the table, so people had to come in turn. I looked out over the congregation: about fifty folk or so. Two sittings. A normal Sunday.

When the first group had celebrated Communion and were returning to their places, I noticed that Robert was in church. Robert was a young man who'd not long ago moved into the parish. He'd been down on his luck, was trying to cope with the break-up of his marriage, and cared for his daughter every second weekend. Rhoda was ten, and Robert was devoted to her. And Rhoda was severely restricted by Down's syndrome. She was apprehensive about leaving her dad, so, when they came to church, she didn't go out with the children to Sunday school, but stayed with Robert in the back row of the church.

This was the first time Robert and Rhoda had been in church for Communion. That's why, when the dozen or so folk remaining had begun to come forward to the table, I was delighted when I saw that Robert was coming too. I could see, however, that Rhoda wasn't happy. She wouldn't let go of her dad. She started to cry. There was the beginnings of a fuss.

I could see one of the church ladies offering to have Rhoda sit with her while Robert came forward for Communion. But Rhoda was having none of it. Then I saw one of the other ladies leaning over to whisper in Robert's ear: 'It's OK to take her with you,' she said (so Robert told me later), 'and I'll come too, if you like.' And, a moment later, I saw Robert coming to the table hand in hand with Rhoda, with a little old lady following close behind.

The three of them took their places. The bread was shared. It came round to the elderly lady first. It could have been passed across Rhoda to her dad. But, instead, it was placed in Rhoda's hands, and, with help, Rhoda took her piece, and then passed the bread to her father.

The cup of wine was passed around the other way; after Robert had taken his sip, he gave the cup to his daughter, who, with great ceremony and with enormous dignity, took a sip as her dad had done, and then passed the chalice, with great care, to the lady on the other side.

That day in the Old Kirk of Edinburgh, I was no longer the celebrant at Communion. The Sacrament was being administered in a whispered conversation by a sensitive lady, by a devoted father and by Rhoda. That day the church was what the Church should be, and the people round that Communion table were truly being Church.

Tom Gordon

DOUBT AND FAITH

(Tune: Fair Helen of Kirkconnel)

Doubt:

This ragtag army, ill-equipped
the power of greed and hate to shift –
how can it hope to play its part
with greed and hate in its own heart?

Angelic natures might contrive
to bring what's lost and dead alive,
but human folk, so prone to sin,
bend with the wind when storms begin!

Faith:

The well-loved Son, when all seemed lost,
left back at base the angel host
and trusted there would come a day
when human beings live God's way.

For God has said: A gamble's on.
I've staked the life of my dear Son.
That ragtag army's what I choose.
The dice is thrown. It's win or lose!

Ian M. Fraser

SONG OF THE LORD'S REVIVING

(after Ezekiel 37)

(Tune: Rustington or Abbot's Leigh)

To death's dark valley God has brought me;
bid me stop and look around:
see the bones of all my people,
strewn and lifeless on the ground;
dislocated, disconnected,
broken signs of hopeless pain:
God now asks of me, mere mortal,
'Can these bones now live again?'

'Lord, that really is my question;
you alone renew the earth;
you can breathe into the lifeless
power to bring them to new birth.'
'Not alone,' the Spirit answers.
'You're not powerless, helpless, weak.
I am with you, I will help you.
Summon courage, dare to speak.'

So I sought the Spirit's presence:
'Blow, creative wind of God:
come to those from life excluded,
send your new life wide abroad.'
Soon the bones are knit together;
soon the sinews strain and strive;
skin and flesh the bones recover –
wondrously, all is alive.

Come creative, moving Spirit,
blow among your people here.
From our lifeless isolation
lead us out and draw us near;
close to you and one another,
close to Christ whose way we tread;
form a people of his purpose,
we his body, he our head.

Leith Fisher

PILGRIMAGE HOME

I called my mum this evening.
Nothing new this Sunday ritual.
Long ago, calls became our weekend routine.

Like times before, we exchanged greetings,
news, love, what we were doing.
Then, her consistent exclamation:
'Your call has made my day.'
Sadness followed.
Not because our call was brief,
nor due to the distance between us.
No, but because my mum won't remember this call.

Usually this does not distress me.
For years now, we have shared her Alzheimer's.
Tonight, however, I wanted her to remember Iona.
Iona, place of memory, island of history,
land of deep roots.
I wanted mum to know I was here.

For centuries, pilgrims have come and gone
from this hard and lovely place.
Her pilgrimage is almost over;
she has come to the edge of being gone,
of coming home.
Still her delight when I told her tonight
will be similar to the joy
when I tell her where I am on Wednesday.

Sometimes pilgrims need neither a history
nor a destination.
Sometimes moments of delight suffice.
I came to Iona to learn something.
I did, now I remember,
call home;
that's where all pilgrimages begin.

Ted Bowman

NOT JUST TO PRAYER AND WORSHIP WE'RE COMMITTED

Words: Ian M. Fraser
Music: Donald Rennie

1. Not just to prayer and wor-ship we're com-mit-ted but, for the strug-gle for a new world fit-ted, 'gainst prin-ci-pa-li-ties and powers we're pit-ted: we're to be church.

Not just in buildings blessed by consecration:
in banks and business, coping with inflation,
and at the office, school and railway station
we're to be church.

Not just on Sundays, festivals observing,
but in the weekdays at a checkout serving,
God looks to us for faithfulness unswerving:
we're to be church

Not just for worship is the promise given;
earth has to be sustained – so that, in heaven,
work linked with prayer together show we've striven
here to be church.

LIVING, LEARNING AND LAUGHING TOGETHER

God of humanity,
we give you thanks for friendships, old and new;
for the opportunity to connect with others,
to share stories and different perspectives,
and to live, learn and laugh together.
Amen

Rowena Aberdeen-de Voil

ANOTHER REJECTION

Another family, another church, another rejection.

My wife, Bonnie, got a call last night from a member of a support group for folk who have a family member with Fetal Alcohol Related Birth Disorders (FARBD). The mother who called is used to dealing with neighbours who don't understand, with teachers who are not sure what to do with her son, with caseworkers who have to be trained by the family – but the church?

Her son, like many folk with FARBD, has trouble with focusing and being attentive, with sitting for long periods of time, with being able to do all the 'normal' things that a person his age can do. So, over the years, instead of being in worship, he has sat in a classroom with other kids, just scribbling and writing and drawing. Not bothering the other kids, not touching them, not being in the way – just sitting there doing his 'paperwork'– in a place where God was, where God's love could be found, where he could find a family. Or so he and his mother had been told.

But now the decision has been made that he should not be 'doing' whatever he does in the classroom. He *should* be in the sanctuary with his mother, he *should* be sitting quietly and attentively, he *should not* get up and wander around. And his mother –

because she has heard all the other stories from all the other families in the support group about their experiences with Church – knows that this is the first step in getting them to leave.

'Oh no,' you will say, 'that's not what is meant. That is not what the leadership of the church is saying.' And I will simply tell you of the dozens of calls I have received (because I am both a pastor and a parent of a child with FARBD) saying that that is how folk with profound disabilities and their families are treated by the Church.

All these folk are 'doing' is looking for a place where they can be accepted for who they are, not judged for who they cannot be; a place where they are loved because they are differently gifted, not ridiculed because they are not bright and healthy; a place where they are affirmed as one of God's children, not condemned because of something someone must have done that was 'contrary to God's will'.

And once again I wished – as I always wish when I hear such sad stories – that I was independently wealthy, so that I could rent a storefront somewhere and start the 'Church for the Broken, the Rejected, the Least, the Lost, the Little, the Ridiculed, the Hurt'.

But isn't that what Jesus Christ tried to start?

Thom M. Shuman

SOMEONE LIKE ME
(A story from Iona)

When we were living at the Abbey, one of the groups who came regularly to stay with the community was from the Six Circle organisation. This movement brought together young men in custody (in those days, in borstal), teenagers under social work super-vision, and folk from a hospital for people with disabilities (in this case, adults with cerebral palsy) for camps each summer, in the belief that living and working with each other would enable each group to learn from the others. One year, the group stayed with us for two weeks – and the magic, as so often on Iona, happened. People who would normally never have thought of meeting each other – never mind beginning to understand each other – gradually became friends – it was so moving to watch, and to be part of it.

On the last evening of their stay, we all shared in the evening Communion service in the Abbey. During the service we shook hands with each other as usual, offering each other a sign of Christ's peace. The service ended and people left; I was the last out of the by then darkened Abbey. I came into the cloisters – and heard the sound of someone sobbing in a corner. When I went over, I found one of the borstal boys, clearly very upset. I went to comfort him, assuming it was because he was having to go back to borstal tomorrow.

'It's not that,' he said, when he got hold of himself. 'It's just that I never thought anyone in a church would ever want to shake hands with someone like me.'

John Harvey

WE OFFER THIS BUILDING

Lord of majesty – we offer this building:
consecrate it to be a place of worship
where your name is exalted
your presence experienced
your power released.

Lord of encounter – we offer this building:
consecrate it to be a place of prayer
where your face is sought
your touch felt
your will revealed.

Lord of the Gospel – we offer this building:
consecrate it to be a place of revelation
where the good news is proclaimed
your word preached
your love shown.

Lord of the Cross – we offer this building:
consecrate it to be a place of reconciliation
where the Body of Christ is restored
barriers are broken down
prodigals return.

Lord of compassion – we offer this building:
consecrate it to be a place of acceptance
where all are welcomed and valued
the rejected find a home
love is poured out.

Lord of the broken – we offer this building:
consecrate it to be a place of healing
where those who mourn are comforted
wounds are tended
lives made whole.

Lord of the oppressed – we offer this building:
consecrate it to be a place of liberation
where the yoke of the past is broken
chains are struck off
people set free.

Lord of the weak – we offer this building:
consecrate it to be a place of empowering
where hearts and hands are strengthened
courage and faith rekindled
the gifts of your Spirit bestowed.

Lord of the redeemed – we offer this building:
consecrate it to be a place of celebration
where bread and wine are freely shared
joy and praise overflow
abundant life is realised.

Lord of Life – we offer this building
and with it our community of faith.
Consecrate them to be a place
where the desert blossoms
and your Kingdom comes!

Pat Bennett

GRAPES

You need the grapes
to make the wine
the grapes that grow
together on the same stem
drawing the same life-giving sap
from the vine
tended by the same vinedresser
but growing together
touching
ripened by the same sun.
Together – in a bunch
shielding each other
protecting each other
supporting each other
yet each grape a complete unity
a whole fruit.
These are the grapes
that make the wine
the joy
the celebration –
these grapes that grow
together.

Ruth Burgess

EMBARRASSED

That's how I feel about being a Christian this week. Embarrassed by the comments of evangelists and megachurch preachers who are going around claiming that Hurricane Katrina is God's punishment on that 'sinful' city called New Orleans. It seems there was an 'unholy trinity' operating down there, comprised of Satanists, voodoo worshippers and homosexuals, according to these folk. I want to ask these folk: 'Haven't you ever read Hosea 11:8–9, or Matthew 7:1–5?'

It's embarrassing – and frustrating.

Frustrating that these are the folk who get quoted by the media, and not the preachers who are talking about compassion, about grace, about the opportunities we have to minister to those in need, just as God asks us. They don't interview the folk in those churches that continue to serve as shelters for the refugees from Katrina. They won't show the father in my congregation who has gone through Red Cross disaster training, and who is leaving tomorrow for three weeks of service in Baton Rouge. They won't feature the youth groups, the ministries, the laity who are out there every day, cleaning and rebuilding and serving meals and mending lives.

It's embarrassing and frustrating.

And I can only begin to imagine how God must feel.

Thom M. Shuman

Appearances

In a burning bush,
a still small voice,
a baby born,
God revealed a Living Presence:
eye-catching, awesome, wonderful.

In nailed hands outstretched,
bread broken, shared,
many fish caught,
Christ revealed a Living Presence:
peace-giving, nourishing, joyful.

In the world's distress,
a friend's loving concern,
another's voice,
the Spirit reveals a Living Presence:
challenging, supportive, leading the Way.

Judith Jessop

I AM

ALLELUIA

Words and music da Noust

2. Come to me, all you who now labour –
   my yoke is easy and my burden light.

3. I am the vine, and you are the branches;
    pruned by my word , you will fruit in me.

4. Feed us all not on bread alone, Lord,
    but every word that's from the mouth of God.

5. I am the way, I am truth, I am life –
    if you know me you will be set free.

GATES AND BREAD

You said you were like
all sorts of things, Jesus:
truth and shepherds,
gates and bread,

and you were –
you are.

When we reckon we've got you all sorted,
sorted and understood,
you smile at us
and give us another picture,
tell us another story,
show us another way.

Live in our lives, Jesus:
be who you are,
who you will be
in us.

Ruth Burgess

I AM THE BREAD

She gave me a loaf of bread,
warm and springy,
labour of love,
the pale crust
dusted with flour.

She gave me the loaf to pray with,
to write about,
to break open –
to share.
I hold it in my hands,
hold the warm, round shape;
feel its gift, its possibilities.

I see in this loaf, a way to be:
hands still with the holding,
heart full with the receiving,
lips parted for the thanking.
I remember the gift of it,
honour the grace in the gift
and the renewing,
as we hold out our hands to receive.

2.

I smell my fresh-baked bread
and the oven where it was cooked.
The bag of flour lies screwed up and empty.
The kitchen is warm;
coffee is brewing

This is the heart of our lives:
the place where we talk,
discuss, explain, listen.

The table is set with plates and knives
and a dish of butter.
This is a place where we share:
we cut slices of bread

and offer them to one another –
slices of warm crumbly bread
to eat with a lump of cheese and tomato.

This is everyday stuff,
everyday story:
bread in the oven,
bread on the wooden cutting board,
bread on our plates –
so common, we talk over it and beyond it;
yet it remains central and (for the fortunate) always there.

Judy Dinnen

THE BREAD OF THE LORD

(Tune: This is the Day/The Lord's Day)

'I am the Bread,
I am the Bread,' Jesus told them all,
Jesus told them all.
'Eat of this bread,
eat of this bread and my life you'll share,
and my life you'll share.'
'I am the Bread,' Jesus told them all.
'Eat of this bread and my life you'll share.'
'I am the Bread,
I am the Bread,' Jesus told them all.

This is the bread,
this is the bread Jesus gives to us,
Jesus gives to us.
Thanks be to God,
Thanks be to God for the life it gives,
for the life it gives.
This is the bread Jesus gives to us.
Thanks be to God for the life it gives.
This is the bread,
this is the bread Jesus gives to us.

'Share out my bread,
share out my bread,' Jesus told his friends,
Jesus told his friends.
Help us to share,
help us to share, Lord, your bread with all,
Lord, your bread with all.
'Share out my bread,' Jesus told his friends.
Help us to share, Lord, your bread with all.
'Share out my bread,
'share out my bread,' Jesus told his friends.

David Hamflett

This song was originally written for an all-age service on the 'I am the Bread of life' saying in John 6, but it could be used at any service of Holy Communion.

WATER OF LIFE

Words and music da Noust

I AM THE VINE

(Tune: Buckland)

Jesus says, 'I am the vine,
rooted deep and growing strong,
bearing grapes that make new wine,
wine to fill the heart with song.

Through the branches runs the sap,
life that vine and branches share;
life that's given to all the world
through the fruit the branches bear.

All who love and follow me
branches are of my true vine,
and my Father prunes and cares
for the branches that are mine.'

Lord, apart from you we're lost,
fruitless branches, withered, dry;
teach us to remain in you,
live the life that you supply.

'You in me and I in you;
share my love, abide in me,
and the good fruit that you bear
shall my Father's glory be.'

Margaret Harvey

THIS DOOR?

I found the door –
Thank God it stood ajar.
Was this the door?
Was this the way?
Was this the entrance through which I am called to go?

I pushed the door,
but it refused to move.
Was this the deal?
Was this enough?
Was this the space through which to squeeze and make my way?

I kicked the door
until my foot was sore.
Was this the style?
Was this the pain,
the pain of never knowing when the door would budge?

I beat the door,
and cursed my God again.
Was this the call?
Was this the voice?
Was this the unknown purpose of this God for me?

I closed the door,
and it slipped shut with ease.
Was this the truth?
Was this the end?
Was this the closure of the way I thought I'd found?

I left the door,
and walked away.
And down the hall another door stood just ajar.
Was this the door?
Was this the chance?
Was this the lesson learned about the way to go?

Another door,
another try.
Was this your door?
Was this your way?
Was this the moment when I would be sure –
my God, your way?

Tom Gordon

HYMN BASED ON THE I AM SAYINGS OF JESUS

(Tune: Carlisle)

O Christ, the heaven-sent bread,
our true life-giving food,
we'll live indeed if we be fed
upon your flesh and blood.

You are the living Vine;
we are your branches, Lord:
We live and grow all linked in you,
made fruitful by your Word.

O Christ, this dark world's light,
the light by which we see
how we may live and walk aright
from fear and darkness free.

O Shepherd of your flock,
our cup with joy you fill;
and though we walk through death's dark glen,
yet we will fear no ill.

Lord, Resurrection, Life,
victorious o'er the grave,
you live in us and we in you –
we trust your power to save.

The Way, the Truth, the Life
which brings us home to God;
we will not fear nor be afraid,
for we walk where you trod.

Ian Cowie

PRAYERS BASED ON THE I AM SAYINGS OF JESUS

Bread

Lord Jesus, your Word is food and drink for us.
Help us to feed upon you day by day
that we may have the strength to do your work.

The Vine

As branches linked together in the Living Vine,
may we be so linked with each other and with you
that our common life may prove fruitful to the glory of God.

Light

Lord Jesus, light up our lives with your love.
Dispel the darkness within us,
and light up the way ahead.

Shepherd

You are indeed our shepherd
so we trust you to lead us through the green pastures of life
and through its dark valleys,
bringing us safely home at the last.

Resurrection

Lord Jesus, we give thanks that now there are no dead ends in life,
and even death itself is an open door.
Put new life into us
and raise us up to new heights of living in this world
and in the next.

The Way, the Truth, the Life

You are the Way into the future
and we will walk your Way of the Cross.
You are the Truth which will never let us down,
and we will trust your Truth.
You are the Life which death itself cannot destroy,
and we will live for you.

Ian Cowie

A DISMISSAL

Leader: Here is the Bread of Life for you.
Give it to others to eat.
(A loaf of bread is given to a member of the congregation.)

Here is the light of Life for you.
Let your light so shine before people
that they may see the lovely things that you do and glorify your Father in heaven.
(A lamp/lantern is given to a different member of the congregation.)

Here is the assurance that the Good Shepherd cares for you.
Nothing can take you from His hands.
(A shepherd's crook is given to a member of the congregation.)

Here is the assurance that death is conquered.
Because He lives, you will live too.
(A Celtic cross is given to a member of the congregation.)

The Vine of His love enfolds you.
Remain in the community of the family of God.
(A bunch of grapes or a Communion cup is given to a member of the congregation.)

Now carry the glory of who He is out into this world –
the world which eats too much and is never satisfied,
while others are left hungry.

Shine His light into the dark places around you;
seek the lost for His sake.

Share the Good News of His death and resurrection with your neighbours.
As part of the living Vine, seek peace and pursue it.

In the Name of Jesus, GO!

The people carrying the symbols process out of the worship area, followed by the rest of the congregation and the worship leader.

Ian Cowie

EUCHARIST, FEASTING
AND CELEBRATION

TAKE, EAT, THIS IS MY BODY

Words and music Carol Dixon

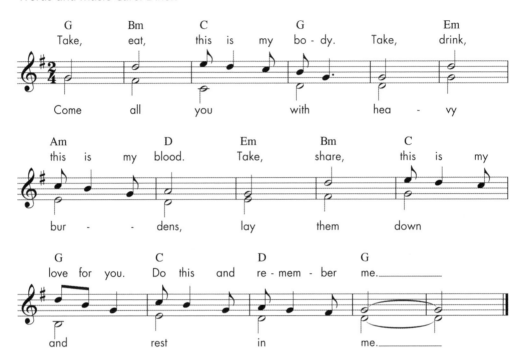

THE FEAST OF LIFE

A service of commitment (Iona Abbey, 1998)

'We are God's guest,' said a pious man of Lewis, 'and 'tis He who keeps a generous table.'

from *Hebridean Altars*

Quiet dinner music is played on a piano as folk enter the worship space.

Welcome *(during which folk greet each other, and exchange stories about a favourite meal. Or, voices like those that follow could be used):*

Voice 1:   My most memorable meal was at college with my housemates. It was the end of the year and everyone had run out of money. So, we decided to throw all the food we had left together, and make a big pot of soup – there was some bread and wine left. We just kept throwing things in the pot –

whatever we could find in the fridge, in the back of the cupboard. When we looked down into it finally, we couldn't stop laughing. It looked revolting! It was a brilliant night though. We just talked and ate soup. Talked about all the funny things that had happened, the serious things. Talked about all we'd shared together during the year. When I speak to those friends now, on the telephone or by email, we all still remember that night. The night that the soup and laughter never seemed to run out.

Voice 2: I remember working in Africa. Being invited to a meal: the incredible hospitality and welcome. A big pot in the middle and everyone sharing. Eating with your hands – the deftness of it. Beans with sauce and bread. On occasions, goat. Drum music and dancing.

Voice 3: My favourite meal was New Year's Day with family. We had fish-fingers, and beans and toast. It was just so relaxed and chilled.

Voice 4: In Peru we were invited to stay with a family, and it was just so nice. It was on an island in Lake Titicaca. Four, five thousand metres high up maybe. They could only grow potatoes up there. Potatoes and some special kind of rice. The mother cooked a meal for us. Just potatoes and rice. So simple. Potatoes from the garden. Nothing fancy. So simple and close to the earth – but it was one of the best meals I've ever eaten. It was just being there: the place where potatoes come from originally. Sitting in the kitchen; the guinea pigs they ate sometimes running around everywhere. The men knitting these beautiful colourful hats and the women carrying sacks of potatoes, walking in sandals made from car tyres. The way they had so many different ways of cooking potatoes. The way their faces were beautiful and furrowed like the earth. Their hands, dark and rough. Like the earth.

Opening responses

God, you have given us all kinds of plants;
those that bear grain and those that bear fruit.
O TASTE AND SEE THAT THE LORD IS GOOD

You have given us your Word and Law sweeter than honey,
sweeter than honey dripping from the comb.
O TASTE AND SEE THAT THE LORD IS GOOD

You have given us manna in the wilderness of our wandering
and our daily bread to sustain.
O TASTE AND SEE THAT THE LORD IS GOOD

You have given us:

The heavenly smell of roasted coffee
and the green, rooted scent of gardens dripping rain

The rush of sugar
and the smack of saltiness

The sea-rounded smooth feel of stones
and the texture of tree bark

The sound of wood thrushes and herring gulls
pianos and choirs
tubas and skirling bagpipes playing drunken reels at parties
O TASTE AND SEE THAT THE LORD IS GOOD

Song: For the fruits of all creation (*Common Ground*)

Scripture reading/drama (based on Luke 14:15–23)

Cast: A waiter and eight dinner guests. The waiter is dressed in a tuxedo or suit and cummerbund.

A table stands in the centre of the worship space set with wine glasses, dinner plates, cutlery, jugs of water, baskets of fruit, a loaf of bread on a wooden sideboard, meadow flowers in a vase ... the table reflecting the bounty and the beauty of God's Kingdom. Unlit nightlights have been placed on each dinner plate. The waiter walks around the table, smoothing out the tablecloth and making final touches. The dinner guests mill about holding invitations.

Worship leader:	Then Jesus said: 'Someone gave a great dinner and invited many. At time for the dinner he sent his servant to say to those who had been invited':
Waiter:	Come, for everything is ready.
Leader:	But they all alike began to make excuses. The first said to him:
Dinner guest 1:	*(addressing the waiter)* I have bought a piece of land, and I must go see it; please accept my apologies. *(Each dinner guest speaks, hands their invitation back to the waiter, and leaves.)*
Leader:	Another said:
Dinner guest 2:	I have just been married and therefore cannot come.

Leader:	Another said:
Dinner guest 3:	*(in a mad rush; carrying a briefcase, juggling papers and a mobile phone)* Sorry, but I have to get back to work. My email's really piling up – and I'm waiting for a very important call. Please understand, but my diary's full ... Oh, and I'm on a diet anyway.
Leader:	Another said:
Dinner guest 4:	Sorry. No, really, thanks, but I've eaten already. I dine at all the finest restaurants, you see – French, Italian, Indian, Chinese, you name it. This is nice – but you should see the wine lists there! Please accept my apologies but I'm full, really. And, to be honest, I don't really think there's anyone coming to this dinner who could improve my chances.
Leader:	Another said:
Dinner guest 5:	Sorry, but I just remembered I forgot to lock all my doors and windows before I came. Oh, and I think I left the cooker on. *(Runs out)*
Leader:	Another said:
Dinner guest 6:	Sorry, but I need to be alone. There are too many people here. There's too much noise. I've got things I need to chew over by myself. I feel crowded. I need my space. Please understand.
Leader:	Another said:
Dinner guest 7:	*(with attitude)* Hey man, I just don't got the time now. Always had trouble sittin' still, know what I mean? Ever since I was a kid. See, I need movement in my life, speed, excitement. I got things to do, places to go, people to see. Sorry, but this kinda thing just doesn't satisfy my appetites, if you know what I mean. Maybe snatch a little bread or something for the road though. Hey, got any crisps? Send me an invite next time though, although I move around a lot.
Leader:	Another said:
Dinner guest 8:	Sorry, but I don't deserve to be here. If you knew my past you wouldn't have invited me in the first place. The things I've said, the things I've done. My thoughts are a feast of terrible things. I'm full of anger and jealousy – and that's just for starters. No, all this colour and bounty and beauty must have been meant for someone

	else, not me. Not me. If you knew the things I've done ... Thank you, but I'm not worthy. *(Shuffles off)*
Leader:	Then the owner of the house got angry and said to his servant: 'Go out at once into the streets and alleys of the city and bring in the poor, the homeless people in shelters, the elderly folk in nursing homes; those who are lonely, those who are grieving, those who are misunderstood.' And the servant said:
Waiter:	Lord, what you have ordered has been done and there is still room.
Leader:	Then the master said: 'Go out into the suburbs and the countryside, to the shopping malls and prisons, to the detention centres and refugee camps, and compel people to come in – all those hungry for justice, hungry for understanding, hungry for the feast of life – so that my house may be filled.'

Prayer of confession

Dear God, we confess how difficult it is for us
to accept your invitation:

Self-absorbed and busy following our own agendas.
Tied up with all our engagements, demands, responsibilities, promises, regrets ...

We confess that we are afraid and anxious,
that we can't sit still with ourselves –

or sit down with others who are different and
who do not like the same things.

And we admit
how difficult it is for us to truly, honestly
taste and swallow this world:

with its rich experiences of sweet and sour,
sorrow and joy;

to live openly and hopefully –
to trust in your grace and believe in resurrection.

Lord God,
help us to say yes to the feast you have prepared for all
to taste and share.

Help us choose life in all its fullness
over substitutes that leave us sick and tired,
empty and wanting.
Amen

The invitation

Leader: Following the next song, you are all invited to come to the table in the
              crossing, and to light a candle at a place setting there. God calls us to
              come taste of the feast of life.

Song: God has a table, *Love From Below*, John L. Bell and Graham Maule,
        Wild Goose Publications

Grace *(Before the action, a table grace is said.)*

Action *(during which quiet dinner music could again be played)*

Prayers of concern *(including prayers for the hungry and the excluded)*

We pray now for those who are without food.

For those dying in famines in Sudan, North Korea ...
On the well-dressed streets of Western democracies.

God in your mercy,
HEAR OUR PRAYER

For those dying of loneliness.

Starving for love and attention in the slums and dumps of hostile cities.
In rich, towered Manhattan, London ...

God in your mercy,
HEAR OUR PRAYER

For those living without the sustaining energy and goodness of your Word.

God in your mercy,
HEAR OUR PRAYER

The Lord's prayer *(said together)*

Closing song

Closing responses

For all that you have given us,
generous, loving God,
WE PRAISE YOU
AMEN

Blessing

Following the service there could be a community meal or a ceilidh.

Marion Brown and Neil Paynter

A FORETASTE OF THE HEAVENLY BANQUET

Not much of a banquet, if the foretaste is anything to go by! A measly piece of bread and a little glass of wine (Vintage No.5 – non-alcoholic).

It's a bit like a party, I explain to the children.

But where's the music to dance to? And the pizza and fizzy drink? Why all the solemn faces and quietness?

Yet the children come closer. They stand with the grown-ups, stifling giggles.

'The body of Christ broken for you. The blood of Christ shed for you.'

'The bread of life given for you. The love of God poured out for you.'

The most experienced child shows the newest what to do. Precious bread is held with studied seriousness. There are nudges and sideways glances. Slurps from the toddler. The wide-awake baby watches her parent, and reaches out for her share. The youngest child, standing knee-high in the circle, asks for more (a grace-full theological response?). The reluctant participant hangs back.

'Here's some for you, too,' I say, inviting him in … 'Would you like some of my bread?'

I like to think that Jesus might have said that as he welcomed the least and the littlest, the lost and the cautious, to his feast.

'Thank you,' they say, as befits a Eucharistic feast.

The food is the gathering point.

The people (a motley bunch) are important ingredients.

Not a bad foretaste after all.

Judith Jessop

THE BREAD AND CUP PASS ME BY

The bread and cup pass me by.
I neither taste nor touch them,
yet each Sunday I breathe them in.

Bread

sour yeast, the smell of past sorrows;
warmth of a freshly baked loaf;
crumbs, fragments of lives brought together;
salt tears for fresh grief.
Dusty flour blanketing tabletops and hands like snowfall.
Wheat grains packed with promise, as blades emerging from the wet earth.

Wine

fermented yeast intoxicating us all;
parties and lazy lunches;
loss and abandonment;
purple grapes pressed for us to celebrate or drown in;
the smell of red;
tasting blood.
Blood spilt for nothing or for everything;
clinical glass cups for our see-through lives.

People

pressed close in a circle or spread along the pew;
breathing in those gathered:
the holiness of which incense is a sign;
the richness of faces, bodies, textures, perfumes, dirt.
Like animals deciphering a scent,
we inhale our fears and faiths
and, like the tide, flow in and out of this place.

Through these long years,
God calls us here.
Some are called to take and break bread and drink wine,
some to be friends amongst strangers,
others to know the place of the stranger, even amongst friends.

And to all God promises: I will not let you go;
God breathes us in, and, together, we conspire.

Rich fragrance, costly perfume fills this place,
drifting out into the fields and streets beyond.

Rachel Starr

BREAD

Words: Pat Bennett   Music: John L. Bell

hun - gry world_ is_ fed._

For, having planted seed corn deep
in every human heart,
there, quickened by affirming grace,
your kingdom's work can start.

I open to your ripening power
the pattern of my days:
the salty sweat of daily work,
my rest and leisure's ways.

I offer to your shaping hands
the stories of my life:
the hopeful lines of joy and faith,
the darker words of strife.

Through all these elemental things,
your leavening power unleash:
transform the textures of my life –
the dough becoming flesh.

Then break me with the hands of grace
that living, I may prove
a generous bread of kingdom life –
of healing, peace and love.

WE'RE LONGING FOR A DIFFERENT WORLD

Words and melody: Ian M. Fraser
Arrangement: Donald Rennie

We're long-ing for a dif-f'rent world where jus-tice is the key and crown, but self-ish claims and world-ly aims con-tin-u-al-ly let us down.

We want it both ways, we confess
to you who are our Lord and King:
a life secure
from living poor,
a life of risk and venturing.

We know that we are not our own
and what we own is really yours,
but we will fight
to hold on tight
to gains which privilege secures.

So here, we pray, take hold of us,
through bread and wine, claimed by the Son:
self's castle storm,
our lives transform,
with Christ's own nature make us one.

POTTER'S HOUSE EUCHARIST

It was time for the Eucharist to be shared. The Word had been offered, and in that remarkable worship setting – Potter's House Community Church in northwest Washington, DC, a coffee shop by day and a worship centre in the evening – there was a palpable sense of expectation.

All the aspects of Potter's House worship were creative and stimulating – from the welcome of strangers to the focus of the message of the leader; from the depth of the prayers to the discussions over a meal … And now the Eucharist was to be the culmination of it all.

I cast my eyes around the table as the Communion elements were being prepared. There were people there I had come to know well in my time in their midst, and people I knew only a little. And there was Gerry.

Gerry was a young man with Tourette's syndrome, and he epitomised for me the nature of 'being Church' in Potter's House. For in his muttering and cursing, his twitching and interrupting, his all-round unpredictability, Gerry was loved and embraced as part of the church. He had his own role to play. He was an integral part of the Body of Christ – and it showed!

And there I was, with Gerry beside me, and I was part of that embrace for him. I was helping him be part of the Church. I could be a part of making the Eucharist work for Gerry. And I felt really good about that.

In time, the bread was shared – in the custom of Potter's House, passed from person to person around the table. The bread came to me from my neighbour on my one side, and, after I had partaken, I passed the Body of Christ to the twitching and cursing Gerry.

'The Body of Christ broken for you,' I said, as I steered the bread into his uncoordinated fingers.

In that moment I was Gerry's minister. I was facilitating the Eucharist for him; I was creating Church for him. And I felt immensely pleased to be able to do that.

I basked in my inner pleasure – until the time came for the chalice of wine to be shared. To my horror, I realised that the cup of wine was coming around the table – the other way! The wine would be passed from the neighbour on Gerry's other side and, through Gerry, to me! A chalice of wine in the twitching fingers of Gerry? The Blood of Christ in such unpredictable hands?

The predicted scene that was forming in my mind was one of unmitigated disaster. Communion ruined. The Eucharist losing its meaning. Worship going dreadfully wrong. Embarrassment all round – and mostly for me … It seemed an age as the cup of wine made its way round the table. Then it was being passed to Gerry. God, not this, not now, not me …

I heard the words, 'The Blood of Christ shed for you', coming from the other side of Gerry, and watched him hold his hands out to take the chalice.

When his fingers closed round the cup, his twitching stopped. He raised the chalice to his lips, and there was no cursing or muttering. He partook of the Blood of Christ, and he was perfectly still. Then, turning to me, Gerry said, 'The Blood of Christ shed for you,' and let go of the chalice into my hands.

As soon as his fingers let go of the cup and it was safe in my hands, Gerry started to twitch and curse and mutter again.

I remember little more of the events of that evening – such was the power of that Eucharistic moment.

But I am left now with one certainty and with many questions. The certainty? I know who was ministering to whom around that table. Gerry was my minister. He was the officiant at my Eucharist. Christ had put his Body and Blood into Gerry's hands so that Gerry could include me in communion with the Body of Christ.

And the questions? Who was the broken person at that Eucharist table? Who was flawed by his arrogance? Who needed to be healed from his certainties? Who needed to be accepted again as part of the Body of Christ? What is 'being Church' really about? What is the true meaning of the Eucharist?

A journey to find the answers began around a table with Gerry in Potter's House Community Church.

Tom Gordon

AND ARE THE BREAD AND WINE YOUR BODY, LORD?

(Tune: Finlandia)

And are the bread and wine your body, Lord,
blessed and transformed to food which feeds the soul,
so that, substantially, we're one with you
and broken lives, in union, are made whole?
Come, Holy Spirit, sanctify this tryst
and enter in to make us one with Christ.

And is the total universe held here
clasped in a web of sacrificial love
whose pulses weave the atom and the sphere
into one tapestry, here and above?
Come, Holy Spirit, sanctify this tryst
and enter in to make us one with Christ.

So frail the symbols, yet in them we see –
through fruit of human labour, bread and wine –
in Christ's own being, ours in mystery,
bone of his bone, flesh of his flesh entwine:
Come, Holy Spirit, sanctify this tryst
and enter in to make us one with Christ.

Thus we need live no longer to ourselves:
indwelling grace gives power beyond our own;
gifts are unleashed to change the universe
that it attain its end through you alone:
Come, Holy Spirit, sanctify this tryst
and enter in to make us one with Christ.

Ian M. Fraser

BIRTHDAY CELEBRATION

Here we are at the heart of things,
celebrating in style
a wonderful person
with companionship and love.

A true eucharist:
a thanksgiving for friendship,
a meal shared,
inclusive and free.

Sitting at wisdom's table
with table talk and song,
laughter
filling the air.

Surrounded by strangers
becoming active participants
in our revelries
and feasting.

Renewing old friendships,
catching up with loving,
not wanting an ending,
enthusing with new beginnings.

Time lingers ...
Making connections:
a round table of love
at the heart of city life.

Colours and cultures,
young and old,
sharing in the liberation
of older years.

Elizabeth Baxter

AT THE GATES

We shared Communion at the gates of Faslane:
one of the places in a broken world
where breaking bread and drinking bitter wine
is most relevant.
We shared it to remember
security – not of barbed wire and missiles –
but of God's love
that risks all and gives life.
We shared, in a warm circle of believers.
But later, when we sat down on the cold road,
we found that the bread and the cup
had escaped, and were still out there in the crowd,
being shared, carefully, among people of all kinds:
this paradox
of pain and promise
being passed from hand to hand
in a broken world.

Jan Sutch Pickard

THE BODY OF CHRIST

Bread and wine
shared upon a ship,
with Africa to the south,
Europe to the north
and Asia eastwards.

The bread unites,
the wine gives life
to all the many varied members
of Christ's body,
when shared in faith.

Bread and wine,
symbols of a life
given in sacrificial love,
uniting Christians
across the world.

Beryl Chatfield

DANCING WITH THE CREATOR

God will dance with joy for you. (Zephaniah 3:17)

God dances with joy for me –
for me?
Then I will dance with joy for him,
and with him.

There are so many different kinds of dance:

The dance of resurrection – joyful, free, abandoned dancing with my risen Lord on beautiful days: watching sunsets, storm clouds and rainbows; feeling the wild wind on the top of a mountain I have climbed. My 'free child' free to dance with the sun – the wind and rain on my face, arms and legs. I whirl round and round until all the colours are mixed up and I am out of breath.

The dance of crucifixion – slow, sad dancing with my Creator as we grieve for the death and abuse of children all over the world, for child soldiers and child prostitutes, for the loss of their innocence and potential. We dance for all the sadness in the world and for the ways in which people maltreat each other; for the lonely, the outcast and the rejected.

The dance of the Furies – a war dance – angry dancing in the battle against racism, sexism, hunger and violence, against exploitation and the treating of people without dignity and respect, as less than human. I dance with anger when the Church stifles growth, honest questioning or exploration of faith, in an attempt to hold control; or when it teaches that God is harsh and judgemental, or that God is static and can be imprisoned and defined.

I sometimes dance a left-brained dance – precision, figure dancing like a Scottish reel – making and enjoying patterns and sequences. Maths and science join this dance: the precision of numbers, flower structures, spirals in seashells and leaves; of shapes, of orbits – atoms and solar systems dance with me.

In my own creativity, I join with the Creator in a right-brained dance as my imagi-nation is allowed to flow freely in words, music, pictures, movement …

But at other times I just want to smooch with my Creator – to accept my tiredness, to abandon myself into his enfolding arms, to rest my head on his loving shoulder, hardly moving, just swaying to the deep rhythm of the music of the universe, not think-ing or doing, just being; not progressing, just resting – content in one another's arms, in mutual love and enjoyment of being together, relaxed, timeless, effortless, not striving, just being.

And one day, when I am tired and the lights are dim, I hope to do the Last Waltz with Jesus – to be held in his loving and upholding arms and hugged, until at last he whispers, 'Shall we go home now?'

Frances Hawkey

THE CUP

As the cup was offered
she took it,
drank deeply
and handed it back
to the celebrant
with a smile,
speaking the ritual words
of her community
'Thanks, Bob.
Cheers!'

Cheer us, friend Jesus:
warm us when we're lonely;
and be the merry-maker
of our nights and days.

Ruth Burgess

COMMUNITY

GLORY TO GOD IN THE HIGH STREET

Words and melody: Ian M. Fraser
Arrangement: Donald Rennie

1. The bread and wine Christ chose were dai - ly ra - tions, sus - tain-ing life for beg-gar as for king; through them he gives him-self and so fa - shions in - to one ta - pes - try each day's off -'ring: thus, through the warp and woof his life sup- plies, we too may suf - fer with him, with him rise.

2. Thus daily life displays Christ's abounding grace
    and nappy-changing is a living sign
    as love matures – yet keeps that tender face,
    when lips caress and loving arms entwine.
    Now resurrection life is all around:
    life's daily tasks and claims are holy ground.

THE CHURCH IN THE COMMUNITY

(A story from the Gorbals)

In 1998, Gorbals Parish Church and Blessed John Duns Scotus Catholic Church took the significant step of signing a joint covenant. Under the terms agreed, both congregations committed themselves to action together in the local community, as a sign of their shared baptism and their common discipleship.

Almost immediately, they initiated 'Bridging the Gap'. Its aim was, and still is, to seek to bridge some of the divides that exist in this Glasgow inner city area, currently undergoing its second 'regeneration' within the past fifty years.

To begin with, the work was with children in the divided school system: teaching them common songs, doing shared drama, putting on joint shows, and thereby, of course, involving parents and grandparents as well.

The work in the schools has since greatly expanded – the project now employs three workers, two full-time and one part-time, running citizenship classes, and working with as many as 70 pupils each year in Peer Tutoring, across two primary and two secondary schools.

Since 2000, the Gorbals has played host to up to 200 asylum-seeker families, dispersed here by the Home Office. 'Bridging the Gap' was asked by the local community to take the lead in welcoming them – and now employs two part-time workers to head up a large team of volunteers, offering daily advice and support and a weekly drop-in.

In recent years, trips have been made both to Iona and to the Corrymeela Community in Northern Ireland; horizons have been broadened, and prejudices uncovered and dealt with. There are, of course, many more divides in the local community; but by working on the basis of what can be done, rather than what can't, the work goes ahead in small but significant ways.

In these ways, the two congregations recognise and support the original aim of the covenant, hoping and praying that they can continue to witness to the Gospel together in this part of Glasgow.

John Harvey

VISION

I'm starting to belong everywhere.

In the place where the sky kisses the sea,
    where the waters' colours meet,
    where your hand touches mine,
    where my darkness lifts,
        where God is within
        and in where God is.

In the place where the wave turns to foam,
    where rock mottles,
    where you enter me,
    where pain can be transformed,
        where God is within
        and in where God is.

In the place where the rain hits stone,
    where water falls,
    where I move outside,
    where forgiveness dawns,
        where God is within
        and in where God is.

In the place where the city starts,
    where the secular is sacred,
    where you welcome me,
    where I know I am healed,
        where God is within
        and in where God is.

In the place where the world becomes church,
    where chancel meets nave,
    where pink runs into purple,
    where queer is not strange,
        where God is within
        and in where God is.

I'm starting to belong,
I'm starting to belong,
I'm starting to belong
          everywhere!

Rosie Miles

ABBOTT AND COSTELLO MEET THE MUMMY

(From a longer story about working in a shelter for homeless men)

Roy comes in in a mellow mood, he's gonna see how it goes. 'That's good,' I say. 'Yeah, yeah, all you can do. Why get all worked up about it?' he says. 'Doesn't do nothin'.'

I nod. He smiles; shakes his head like life's fuckin' crazy but he's still hanging in there. 'One day at a time,' he says.

I ask him how his day went. He was over at the Work Programme.

'Well, not all day. Just from ten 'til two. That's all they can keep it open for.' He wishes they could keep it open all day. 'They're lookin' for funding.'

Roy makes trophies out of wood.

'Not easy sometimes with this but' – and lifts up his clawed right hand, paralysed from a knife fight. I can't imagine anyone having the guts to pull a knife on Roy: two hundred pounds solid – easily.

'Severed the tendons and shit … Yeah, but you shoulda seen the other guy! Let's just say he ain't walkin' too well.'

When his low-income housing comes through he can get out of here; go to the Work Programme days and make trophies. He'll get faster at it, he says.

'I have no doubt,' I say.

'Oh, neither do I,' says Roy, 'neither do I.'

His girlfriend's living with her mother for now. She's not drinking as much.

'That's great!'

'Yeah.'

Before the baby she drank like no tomorrow. Two forty ouncers a day. Roy says he's anxious to move in with her again and start a new life, but he knows it's gonna take time. 'So, the social worker in tonight? Oh no, that's next week, right? Oh well, it can wait, it can wait. No point gettin' all worked up.'

They're thinking of taking Sticks in too; getting a place with an extra room or a pull-out or something. Sticks hitched with him all through the States.

'Crazy – yeah, but it's only if he can get off the coke first. That's the condition. 'Cause it's just gonna bring us all back down I know.' Roy glances up at me. 'He still feels like a brother, no matter what. Know what I mean?' he asks.

I nod.

'Well, it'll work itself out. One day at a time,' he says. 'So, those movies?' he asks.

Things in the common room are mellow. No fights or arguments.

Someone says should have got *Silence of the Lambs*. 'Guy fuckin' eats people.'

'No, or a porno,' someone else says.

Ollie picked up some classic old comedies. Down at Video Busters. 'Something silly. Give the boys a laugh for a change.' The Keystone Cops, Laurel and Hardy. And for the main feature: *Abbott and Costello Meet The Mummy*.

The door buzzer rings (it's Duane I can tell). At the inside door he hands over his switchblade, and some supplies he picked up at the five-finger discount: red liquorice, Maltesers, and a jar of Orville Redenbacher Gourmet Popping Corn – produces them, like a magician, from bottomless coat pockets.

'Hey, need some help there, dude?' he calls over to Dave, my colleague, who's having trouble with all the wires, fuckin' wires, in back of the TV.

'Hey, don't let him go anywheres with that VCR, eh,' somebody says.

'Yeah, watch the back door.'

'Relax,' says Duane. 'Take a downer. Take a break.'

'We got movies? Movies tonight?' someone asks. And as I go answer the door again I can smell popcorn popping.

'Hey, tell him tons of butter. Tons!'

On the way, I pass by Henry, sitting with his arm round Lola: a life-size – and life-like – blow-up doll he bought at a sex shop downtown.

I pass Joseph, and ask him how he's doing.

Joseph used to be a student but dropped out – 'One day finger math will be faster than a computer' – graduated here. The professor, they call him. He still carries his brief-case around with him everywhere; wears thick, black-framed eyeglasses held together with electrical tape and a University of Toronto sweatshirt he refuses to change.

'I'm still trying to figure out the epsilon; still working on Pascal's triangle and the repeating enigma of pie. It's all a chess game, it's all a chess game, it's all a game.'

He doesn't have time for a shower.

'Time's a hole you could measure with formulas,' he answers, pacing, his hair out at angles.

He sits down periodically, to play chess with The General. I played him myself one night and he beat me in six moves! I sat dazed, wondering.

'One day finger math will be faster than a computer. I'm still working on the epsilon, the enigma, pie, it's all a chess game – an abacus, an abyss, an arboretum …'

The door again. I peer out through the Plexiglas. Tommy. So I buzz him in.

'Oh boy, oh boy, no more hot water left now, I'll tell ya.'

Tommy loves coming in after being out all day and jumping in a nice hot shower. Sometimes you can't get him out, with him singing and splashing around.

He strides and paces, his big ears sticking out. 'Oh boy, no more hot water left now, I'll tell ya,' rubbing his cold hands together now like he's about to run and dive in; but before he does he plunges into the common room to see his friends. Pals he's known since grade school – Sylvester, Jake, Danny. The gang of them hang out in the park and pass the bottle round. Shoot up. But no one's in yet.

'Hey, where is everyone? … Where's mom? Ollie The Trolley?'

The buzzer rings again – and it's a fancy, fur-lined woman with leftovers from an office party. Her arms are full and Tommy runs to help her.

'There's more in the car,' she sings, and Duane jogs out, while Tommy fumbles and juggles the cases and plastic trays to the kitchen like slapstick.

There are little quarter cut sandwiches, chips and dips, a couple cases of Schweppes ginger ale, cheese platters …

'Oh boy, there's a mouse in the house. A mouse in the house now, I'll tell ya.'

Ollie comes out of the kitchen wearing a *Simpsons* apron.

'Ollie The Trolley, Ollie The Trolley!'

Ann steps out of her office.

'Mom!'

She stands on her tiptoes and gives Tommy a big hug. He's six-foot-three, and they dance.

'Mom.'

Many nights she's the first person Tommy asks for in the door. Nights when he staggers in clutching his heart; nights he shivers and trembles and cries.

She cradles Tommy's cold hands and asks him where his mittens are.

Ollie says: 'See, God answers prayers,' and rearranges the crackers and marbled Colby cheese, the celery and carrot sticks, picking out the wilted lettuce, filling in the holes, making everything nice.

'Hey, movies tonight, Tommy. We got movies. Videos.'

Tommy blinks.

'Hey, maybe we shoulda got a Western too. A Western for Tommy.'

'Next time. Have a video night regular.'

'Yeah, that's what I was thinkin'.'

'Got a membership card.'

Tommy suddenly starts slinking and slanking around the OK Corral of a lobby, under the fluorescent high noon lights, hands in his pockets, jingling and jangling and the change he made out on the square begging.

Tommy can remember every character in *Gunsmoke*, *Bonanza*, *Have Gun Will Travel* … Remembers when he was a little boy: lying on the rug in the basement of his mother's house, watching television. Says to ask him a question, ask him a question; peers at us – steely-eyed; starts singing theme tunes, galloping through them. Then turns and points and fires. Fires – and so I stagger around the lobby like I've been shot, caught in an ambush.

'Gotta cha. Oh boy, got cha, got cha.'

But then I turn, and point, and fire – and Tommy acts like he's taken a silver bullet in the chest. Lurches and clutches his heart, staggers and turns in circles. And as I watch him die slow I remember he *is* dying, of AIDS. Tommy has AIDS and is slowly dying. Mr Johnson signals me over after the dust has cleared and Tommy has gone upstairs.

'I just wanted to tell you that I think you are a nice person. Well, that's all that I wanted to say,' he says. 'You remind me of my brother. He lets me get away with murder too. Lets me in when I've been drinking. But I've made up my mind – this has *got* to stop. I'm gonna get a job. Well, that's all I wanted to tell you.'

Mr Johnson spends his afternoons down at the drop-in centre, leafing through the classifieds while secretly sipping tall cans of Strong Brew he hides in coat. Once he worked hundred-and-fifty-foot cranes. Massey Ferguson bulldozers. Built skyscrapers, moved the earth. Now he stops outside the offices and towers he built, and sits and watches people going in and out.

In the springtime he'll go down and see what's doing, he tells me. 'There's no point before,' he says. 'When the weather gets better. In the spring. There's no use gettin' all worked up about it … I used to operate bulldozers. Cranes. Did I tell you? In the springtime they'll be loads of work. That's when things get movin'. There's no point before – Christ's sake, there's still six feet of snow out there,' he laughs, and glances up at me … 'But I know,' he says soberly, 'this has *got* to stop.' And he shakes his head like he's trying to clear it. 'You remind me of my brother. I never really thanked him. He has a wife, kids – I'm here.' Mr Johnson looks around the smoky, crowded room of men; throws up his hands.

'Well, I just wanted to say that I think you are a nice person.'

I thank Mr Johnson, and tell him that I think he is a nice person, too.

There's a silence, and I ask him if he wants to come and watch some movies. 'Ollie's got movies.'

'Movies? … Movies?' he laughs. 'Sure, why not?'

'Why not.'

'When summer comes I'll go down. See what's doing.' He glances at his wrist-watch; stands up and sways, then sits back down. Waits until the lights go out before he lifts himself up again.

'Hey man, hit them lights!'

'Yeah, make it like a real movie. Like a real movie would.'

Men start drifting over – drawn by the unbelievable smell of hot buttered popcorn. Men who were sitting playing solitaire; men who were comatose.

'God, I thought I was dreaming. Dreaming that smell.'

'Hot buttered popcorn,' mumbles Duane, stuffing his face. And pretty soon we've got

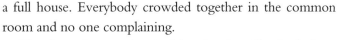

a full house. Everybody crowded together in the common room and no one complaining.

The front door again. And by the time I'm back from handing out peanut butter and jelly sandwiches to a hungry family of five, the first feature is rolling.

There's a miraculous feeling of tired bodies relaxing as the long day unwinds, of the men slowly letting down their guards while, through the grilled windows, the sun melts over the snowy city.

Marco's here, sitting in a corner. It's great to see him. Usually he paces and paces and can't sit down.

One night shift we were talking, and Dave was saying that it looked to him like Marco was running away from something. 'Maybe he's the one who stabbed and killed that prostitute? You never know.'

Ollie was saying that he was reading about Marco's home country in the newspaper, and about the death squads there in the 1980s, and that maybe Marco had been through something terrible like that, had seen things he was finding it hard to live with.

I was thinking maybe.

Or maybe it was death squads inside his head, because when I'd ask Marco if I could help him somehow, he'd stand and shake his head violently back and forth, back and forth, like he was trying to scatter them, throw them off – my voice just another in the onslaught.

It's great to see him, sitting enjoying some escape, peaking through the tangled vines of his hair, his leg pumping like a jackhammer.

'Hey, who's throwin' popcorn?' Roy suddenly threatens. 'I'm warnin' ya pal, payback's a bitch.' But he's not really serious.

In *Abbott and Costello Meet The Mummy*, the mummy gets all unravelled and one of the men kids: 'Hey, that guy looks a lot like Duane in the morning.'

'Yeah, right, eh,' Duane says, 'dream on. Looks like your mama.'

'Hey, down in front, down in front. Shhh, fuckin shhh,

ha, this part.'

It's good to sit with the guys. A lot nights I stand ready to jump in between them before tempers erupt and fists fly; some nights it's like the Wild West, my body charged with the tension.

Someone pings me in the head – and I'm suddenly caught in the crossfire of a popcorn fight. Duane and Roy; Kahil and The General, but a truce is quickly called …

'Hey, pass that bowl down here, will ya? Stop hoggin' it.

'Cheques in this week, eh?'

'Shut up – movie.'

'Cheques in?'

'Shhh, yeah.'

Roy smiles up at the screen; shakes his head like life's fucking crazy but he's hanging in there, even starting to enjoy it a little.

'Too much salt, my lips,' pants Duane, gulping down cold ginger ale.

'So, good movie, Joseph?'

Joseph has stopped trying to solve the enigma of pyramidal forms, pie and the epsilon for a time and is sitting laughing at someone who got a pie in the eye. He laughs out loud. Like a great bird. Everyone turns and looks at each other. Like a great bird.

'Lemon pie in the eye, oh boy.'

Ollie stands in his *Simpsons* apron, holding the trays the angel brought. 'Half-time,' he announces, and there's a polite push.

In the back row Henry's got his arm around Lola, pulling her close, making his move.

Someone has given old Willie a cigarette. A clean, white cigarette: not a rollie, not a dirty, stamped-on butt. He smokes with his tired eyes closed, the calm, quiet dark washing over him; he exhales, and the smoke swirls and hangs.

Tommy stands underneath the ceiling, nibbling crumbly old cheddar cheese, colby, broken Wheat Thins … 'Oh boy, there's a mouse in the house, a mouse in house now I'll tell ya …'

Roy chews on a cocktail stick, puts his feet up.

Back in the kitchen, Ollie's popping up the Orville Redenbacher and whistling It's a Long, Long Way to Tipperary. There's an explosion of laughter, and we turn and look at each other.

Neil Paynter

THE TOUCH OF GOD

A mother's hand cradling the head of her newborn baby:
I am supporting you all the time. You cannot fall.
A father's finger clasped in the grip of his infant's hand:
making an eternal connection.
A mother's hand on the fevered brow of her ill toddler:
The healing power of God moving through me to you.
The gentle stroking of a parent's hand on the arm of a drowsy child:
I am accompanying you to sleep, stroking away your cares.
The strong handshake between father and high school son:
I honour your growth towards individuality.
The interlocked fingers of two lovers walking along the shore:
Lives intertwined.
A long hug from a parent at the start of a journey into marriage:
I let you go – freely.
A hand resting on another's shoulder:
You are not alone – I am beside you and I affirm you.
The gentle stroking of a wife's hand on the face of her seriously ill husband:
I am with you all the time through all of this.
The casual, passing touch of a couple in their 80s:
a movement into a deeper love.
The final welcoming touch ...
of God.

Paul Heppleston

DURING A POWER CUT

God, thank you for showers and kettles,
for hairdryers, lights, heaters and cookers.
Thank you for the comfort we normally live in.

We pray for the future of our world
as we exhaust gas supplies
and as our power stations come to the end of their lives.
Help us to live wisely and in tune with the earth,
and to educate our children to care for your creation.
Amen

Carol Dougall

THE CHANCE TO MAKE A DIFFERENCE

Creator God, we thank you for the opportunity we have to share this world,
for everyone and everything you created,
and for the chance to make a difference.

Paul Richardson

ESME AND PETER

(from a longer piece about working as a companion/aide)

I've been visiting an elderly couple from 9:00 am until 9:00 pm every day for the last few weeks.

Peter has dementia and Esme's got cancer. Her whole, small shrivelling body racked with the fucking disease. Peter is not very lucid, though once in a while we'll have a short conversation. Or he'll surprise me, suddenly ejaculating: 'Well, let's not sit here all night like dead dicks, boy, let's go for a stroll!'

So, we stride over to the magnificent glittering shopping mall. Peter is a towering, robust old man. We scratch puppies behind the ears in the Little Pals Pet Centre, have a styrofoam coffee in the Food Court, then slowly, silently amble home. I make him his dinner, heaping his plate full because I feel death all around me. Yellow niblits of canned corn, a heap of frozen peas and carrots – even though he only eats his meat and rice pudding. His plate full of colour, grey death all around. After dinner, Peter may bring out a photo album full of old friends and places mostly new to him now. He sits in his chair with the television going, turning the thick pages, yellow photographs falling out onto the green shag. 'It's all right, Peter,' says Esme when he gets confused and upset, speaking his name softly. 'It's all right, dear,' struggling, pulling herself up with atrophied muscles and the trapeze bar. 'It's really all right,' until his face relaxes that awful look of panic and fear and Esme can collapse and close her eyes and breathe. And Peter comes over to the death bed we set up in the living room and bends way down to give her a little hug she can feel in the marrow of bones that ache.

Every evening at twilight, Peter stands gazing out the back window, waiting for the grey squirrel to come to the little tree. Chuckles when it does, when it looks around, eating the walnuts he cracked and left for it. 'Better find somewheres for winter, boy,' he tells him. The backyard squarely fenced, the maple tree dead centre, a puddle of yellow leaves spreading from its bole, flowing out over the tired grass, rippling in a gust.

At eight o'clock, the last stretch before Denny, their son, gets home, I remind Esme to take her morphine. It pours thickly from the jars the nurse leaves in a row like days. Is sickeningly sweet, Esme says, so she mixes it with the Welch's grape juice I go get her. Esme wakes every ten minutes. Seldom gets a good rest now, yet still manages to smile. Sometimes, I slowly crank the bed up and we talk a little after Peter's gone off to sleep – in his clothes, in his hard shoes. About when she was a young bride and he was off to war for five years. Yes, it was lonely she says, but it was worse for him. 'I had Denny then … No man should have had to see the things that Peter did.' He wrote her letters, telegrammed when he could.

She nods off in middle of the story, in the middle of a sentence. I make her coffee and a toasted tomato sandwich. She falls asleep with the sandwich half-eaten in her skeleton hand. I slip it out from between her long fingers, trying not to wake her. Put it back on the plate that comes out of the kitchen cupboard cold. The strawberry-flavoured energy drink I pour and leave on her bedside table is thick with vitamins, is the colour of her cotton jumpsuit she sometimes finds hot, and sometimes finds cold. Wisps of winter-white hair stick up around Esme's flowery kerchief. Her skin has yellowed, is translucent and veiny. Her smile grows more and more distant. Awake or asleep, seems to speak softly of acceptance. There are a couple pictures on the knick-knack-cluttered mantelpiece of her when she was healthy. Wearing make-up and a pinched look. Peter stands impassive in uniforms – Army, Legion, the Greyhound Bus Company

On Friday I came to the house to find Esme's hospital bed folded up like a dead leaf. On the stormy night before she'd been taken to the General.

I returned Monday to learn she'd passed away. I used to bring her garden flowers. Souvenirs of the walks Peter and I took in the park, where broken brown glass glints in cold sun and the occasional condom lies in a shallow puddle, muddy water reflecting a cloudy sky. She used to try to get up and water her plants. I was scared she'd fall and break her hip. 'I'll do it for you, Esme,' I'd tell her. 'It's OK, I'll do it.' Sometimes she'd make it. Sometimes she'd pull herself around with her walker and water her plants; talk to them in a soft, hoarse voice. Rub grey dust off broad, mottled leaves. I'd run and get her knitted shawl. By the end, in the hospital, she slept all day and felt little pain, they said. Body and mind floating in a sea of morphine.

A few days before Esme was taken away to the hospital, I remember Peter looking gently down on his shrunken wife sprawled on the wrinkled bed, and turning and whispering hoarsely: 'Whenever my wife gets sick that woman lying there comes to take her place.' He then went and made us, three people, four cups of instant coffee, one for 'that woman there'.

Now, pacing the creaking, warped floors sensing something is terribly wrong, Peter says, 'Geez, I wish she'd call and let me know.' I ask him if he wants to go for a stroll, see what's happening over at the mall. 'I don't understand it,' he says, 'she just went out for a few things. That's not like her.' And he goes and lies down again. I put one of Denny's happy movies on. *South Pacific*. It seems so fucking surreal – people dancing around on a colourised beach, washing their long, beautiful, thick blonde hair. Denny'll be home soon, I tell Peter. He asks for his son like a little boy restless for the security of his father working late.

'Soon, not too long.'

Peter's heavy steps echo, echo because Denny has started selling the furniture.

Peter will be placed in a nursing home in a few weeks. Over a can of Old Milwaukee at the kitchen table, Denny explains that he'll get better care there. 'I mean you've done a great job, don't get me wrong.'

The fridge whirrs, windows rattle. We sit with our thoughts. In a couple weeks won't have a job, I think; but that is life too.

Neil Paynter

WHO AM I TO GET IN YOUR WAY, MY GOD?*

The homeless, the hungry,
the poor:
always complaining
about their circumstances –
why can't they pull themselves
up by their bootstraps
like I did?

Yet,
you hold open the doors,
waving them in, saying,
'Welcome! There's room
for all.'

I wish people
would stop whining and crying
because life is so unbearable;
but
you reach out:
you touch their wet cheeks
with nail-scarred hands.

Desperate travellers
searching for one
who has living water
get in my way
as I hurry through life;
and
you remove the stones
in their path.

Who am I
to get in your way,
my God?

Amen

Thom M. Shuman

*Acts 11:17 (GNB)

WELCOME EACH OTHER

(Tune: Slane)

Welcome each other as he welcomed you,
sharing your life to the glory of God.
Live in a spirit of covenant love.
Welcome each other as Christ welcomed you.

da Noust

GERRY

People called you

lazy
weak
a loser
fucked in the head

I used to think

if you were missing an arm or leg
if you had been hit by a truck
or had come back from a war

if you had a disease like cancer

they would have felt sorry for you
they would have looked on you as a hero

They would have been more forgiving of you
sittin' there on a bar stool all day long
drinkin' their hard-earned taxes
They would have bought you a beer

(Sometimes they did buy you a drink

when they were feeling superior and generous
during lulls in real life when they came slumming
when they needed to stand beside you in order to get
a taller measure of themselves

When they were down and needed some understanding

Besides
you were a good drunk
You were harmless)

Gerry

you lived across the street
with your mom and dad

'Forty-three years old and still
living with his parents'

You never said much
but when I was growing up you lent me record albums
Paul Simon's *Still Crazy After All These Years*
Imagine by John Lennon

They said a lot

One day
you took me into your father's dark shed
which smelled of gasoline and grass clippings
(you cut lawns sometimes, did odd jobs)
and you showed me your wood carvings:

a timber wolf
a Canada goose
an old man with a cane
the face of a Native American woman

carved from pieces of driftwood you collected and
branches broken in storms
Sunlight came streaming in through the single window
and I saw you in a different light

You looked transformed
ascetic

Your work was beautiful and skilful

I said you should sell some
You said you didn't want to sell them. They weren't that good
They *were* good, I said
They were

You smiled
and looked satisfied for a moment

When I was older I used to see you
down at The Dominion Tavern on Saturday nights
You stayed over on 'the dead side',
with veterans sitting alone at sticky tables
and other old people
life had passed by and
left tangled in cobwebs

Sometimes I'd come over and talk to you

Once on your birthday
you gave me some advice:

Don't grow up like me, you said –
and looked me in the eye

Ah, come on, I said
Come on

I wanted to get back to the music and lights
back to my friends
(back to 'the land of the living')
Everybody was there
The Bar Flies were playing
Layla Tajanii was dancing
in the close, summer heat

I stayed a little longer
and left an empty bottle beside you on the bar
I'd come back later to make sure you got home all right
I told myself
When I remembered
you were gone

Gerry
I heard you killed yourself

Slit your wrists and in a park one night

(Someone walking their dog found you)

Ray the bartender told me when I came back to town one year

I ran into him walking down by the river
The Dominion was a steakhouse now
'Christ, I felt sorry for the kid,' he said.

'Did anyone keep his wood carvings?' I asked.
'His *what*?' he said.

Gerry, I wish I could have said something to make you believe
you weren't a failure in life

Gerry, you touched me –
I wish I could have told you that

Would it have been enough?

I doubt it
I'm sure it wouldn't have. It never is

Gerry, I think you were heroic
to try to transform your great pain

Strong
to have lasted as long as you did

Gerry,
this world is crazy
can't see
the potential beauty
in brokenness

Neil Paynter

THE LONG LONELINESS

Words: based on a quote by Dorothy Day
Music: da Noust

love comes from com - mu - ni - ty – the tell-ing place of truth.___ And

truth heals a com - mu - ni - ty: the tell - ing place of love.

oh___ oh oh___ oh___ oh...

FAIR EXCHANGE

Leader: The Spirit of God has spoken.
            This is what God asks of you:
            Act justly, love tenderly, walk humbly.

Approach

For our failure to act justly:
LORD, HAVE MERCY *(or a sung kyrie)*

For our community's failure to love tenderly:
CHRIST, HAVE MERCY.

For our society's failure to walk humbly:
LORD, HAVE MERCY.

Gospel reading: John 2:13–22

Reflection:

Jesus upset the tables of the moneychangers, overturning the values of their world. The passion of his anger, so close to the Holy of Holies, scandalised those who took responsibility for the house of God. They hated him for it. They wanted him dead.

The prophet in Jesus saw in their response a sign of both his own death and the destruction of the Temple. But Jesus kept trusting God to bring life, even out of death. Only God could raise the body – the new temple – to the new life of glory. If we believe, we too will see the glory of God this Easter season. We too will have our bodies transformed. No longer will our bodies be like the old temple – the place where we used to drive a bargain in our transactions with others to enjoy power over them. No, our bodies will become places in which we freely share the Spirit of love, justice and tenderness – the spirit of a joiner's son. For the body is a place of communion.

Affirmation:

WE WILL NOT TRUST IN WEALTH:
WE WILL SEE THAT WE DO NOT PILE UP MORE POSSESSIONS.

OUR TRADE WILL BE FAIR,
FAIR TO PEOPLE WHO ARE POOR.

Blessing:

May the Spirit of God heal our bodies
and make them places of communion.
May the breath of God heal our hearts
and set them on fire for justice.
May the Spirit of God heal our nation
and make all exchanges fair.

da Noust

CREATION AND NEW LIFE

FINGERPRINTS

Our knowledge of
balloons
magnets
dissolved gases
metal refining
geology
music
rivers
fireworks
gravity and
radio waves
leaves us, especially the scientists, asking,
'Who breathes life into these equations?
Whose fingerprints are these?'

Just as the potter leaves fingerprints in the clay,
so God's fingerprints are all over creation.

David Hawkey

LIFE ON IONA AFTER WINTER

God
thank you for the miraculous awakening of life after winter.
Thank you for the wintering wild geese
for sturdy spring flowers
for the advent of cream teas at the Argyll Hotel.
Thank you for the dawning of a new season.

Simon de Voil

NEW LIFE

A meditation

The apple tree and the fennel plant grow side by side, next to a fallen tree trunk.

The winter was long and all three looked dead for many weeks. Only dry brown could be seen.

But now the days are growing longer and the sunshine warmer. Spring is in the air. New life stirs, almost imperceptibly, irrepressibly.

Along the brown twigs of the apple tree, buds swell and burst open, displaying tiny green leaves and a hint of blossom promising fruit to come. Sap rises from the no-longer-frozen roots, coursing up and out to the furthest tips of the tree, bringing new life to its dormant cells.

The fennel is just as surely awaking with a throb of new life. Feathery green shoots thrust up from deep down at the base of the plant. The old twigs, dry and rigid, are now an encumbrance, cluttering and hampering the new growth yet unable to prevent it. They need to be cut away to free the new.

And new life is starting to colonise the dead tree: in the crevices of its bark, a bracket fungus here, moss there; a clump of grass in a hollow; ivy curling round the dead branches. Even a primrose, its seed planted by some bird, shows its leaves and buds. Micro-life and mini-beasts are using the stored food, breaking down the old cells; insects feed and shelter; birds peck at the rich supply of grubs.

In the Creator's scheme of things, nothing, not even death, is wasted.

What opens me to allow the new, thrusting, pulsating life of Christ to flow freely in and out through me?

What in my life hampers or stifles new life and growth?

What brings me to life – encourages me to take risks, to change to grow?

Frances Hawkey

PROMISE OF SPRING

Spring is struggling this year;
as we wait for skies to brighten,
longing for light and warmth
to restore vitality to our lives:
IN THE TENTATIVE STIRRING OF HOPE
WE LOOK FOR THE PROMISE OF SPRING.

The trees are still wintry,
branches bare, buds tightly closed;
we search for the hint of green
signalling the renewal of the earth:
IN THE TENTATIVE STIRRING OF HOPE
WE LOOK FOR THE PROMISE OF SPRING.

Birth is a hard business
for lambs emerging in the bleak fields;
their plaintive bleats echo
our own cries of vulnerability.
IN THE TENTATIVE STIRRING OF HOPE
WE LOOK FOR THE PROMISE OF SPRING.

New beginnings are not easily won;
we wait, look, listen
for the restless pulsing of new birth
to transform our lives with joy.
IN THE TENTATIVE STIRRING OF HOPE
WE LOOK FOR THE PROMISE OF SPRING.

Jan Berry

A HYMN OF THANKSGIVING FOR LAMBING

Words: Margaret Harvey   Tune: Ave Maria Lourdes

1. Sing thanks for the spring-time, the won - der of___ birth, For lambs in the mea - dow and new green of___ earth.

Chorus

For all the hope of life that is new, We sing, dear Lord, our prais - es to___ you.

2. For harvest of lambing we give you our praise.
   We ask you to bless all our work night and day.
   For all the hope of life that is new,
   we sing, dear Lord, our praises to you.

3. Lord Jesus, good Shepherd, you care for your sheep,
   you feed us and lead us and in safety keep.
   For all the hope of life that is new,
   we sing, dear Lord, our praises to you.

4. Lord Jesus, your blood was for love of us shed.
   We praise you, our Shepherd, raised up from the dead.
   For all the hope of life that is new,
   we sing, dear Lord, our praises to you.

CREATION

Breath of God
surrounding, enveloping,
dancing, nurturing,
holding
the dark and the light,
all colours
and none,
exploding, imploding
the new and the old,
surfacing,
flowering,
living and dying,
held.

Julia Brown

DAFFODIL

on the little coffee table
a new bright sun
is about to burst forth
in petalled rays of yellow

it will give a little light.

Liz Knowles

MAY GOD'S SPRINGTIME SURGE THROUGH ME

A day in early spring.
A sort of thrill hangs in the air.
Life seems to be waiting, expectant, vibrant.
Anticipation is everywhere;
everybody, everything, everywhere feels poised.
What will the new season hold?
Who will come?
What will happen?

In households, guesthouses, hotels, places of pilgrimage
folk spring-clean, take stock,
ready for guests, volunteers, visitors.
Shop windows fill with merchandise.
Boatmen repair and paint their boats.
Farmers plough and plant.

Dormant seeds start to germinate.
Buds start to swell.
Snowdrops thrust through the cold earth.
And daffodils show their gold.
Ewes and cows are heavily pregnant.
Rooks build their nests in tall trees,
and small birds search for hidden nesting sites.

All of creation is hard at work to be ready in time.
So much eager energy.
So much willing toil.
So much necessary preparation.
So much sheer excitement!

May I start each day with as much anticipation and energy.
May I put this much anticipation and energy into life itself.
May God's springtime surge through me.

Frances Hawkey

SUN SONG

(for a rainy day)

I wish I could rip the clouds down
Like damp old wallpaper
And throw them away,
Strip it down to the shell,
The bare husk of the sky,
And start again
With a bigger, brighter sun
And a newer, richer blue.
　　Sun, shine on me
　　Shine on me, Sun
　　Come, shine on me
　　And melt my ice away.

Liz Knowles

A PRAYER ON A WET DAY

Loving God,
Creator of water
on which all life depends,
we are close to you on this wet day.
Thank you for the rain
which softens and refreshes the earth,
making springs rise and streams flow.
Thank you for rivers, lakes and oceans,
and for all that lives beside them and in them.
Thank you for all that is green and growing.
Thank you for the rain, on which our food depends.

Thank you for the water in our taps.
We pray for all those in drought-stricken lands,
where women trudge many miles for water and men toil on barren land.
Thank you for clean water.
We pray for those whose water is contaminated, bringing disease and death.

Thank you for the rain washing the earth,
cleaning the air in the cities,

sparkling as jewelled droplets in the sun,
bringing out the deep colours in rocks and stones.

Thank you for warm clothes and dry houses.
We pray for all who are living rough or in inadequate
housing.

Thank you for the rain without which there would be no
rainbows!

Forgive us when we grumble or complain on wet days.
Forgive us when we only want sunshine in our lives.
Forgive us when we take for granted and waste your life-
giving water.

So, our loving Creator, thank you for this wet day. Amen

Frances Hawkey

IT ALL HAS TO DO WITH

It all has to do with a scientific thingamabob called bio-
luminescence, which refers to thingamajig cells which
contain a whatsit called luciferin.

This whatsit can somehow make a whosit called
luciferase which, when combined with oxygen, makes a
whatchamacallit commonly known to us all as oxyluciferin.

And, of course, it all has to do with sex!

At least, that's what the scientists tell us when we
wonder how and why fireflies light up on a summer
evening.

Me?

I just let them light my way home from a late meeting at
the church and whisper, 'Wow!'

Thom M. Shuman

ROGATION DAY

'This is Rogation Day,'
the preacher announced
before the Sunday service.

Eastertide has come and gone,
five weeks since,
and those familiar days,
with their familiar names,
Palm Sunday,
Maundy Thursday,
Good Friday,
Easter morning,
have had their time,
and in their familiarity
have offered me
the safety and security of faith.

Even Low Sunday
has had its day.

But now,
post-Easter,
beyond secure familiarity,
what is this strangeness
which I have stumbled upon –
this 'Rogation Day'? ...

It is,
I now learn,
a time of penitence,
when I must seek forgiveness
from my God,
that he might bless the land
for what is yet to come.

God's forgiveness
to bless my land?
The healing of my brokenness
to influence now

the growing of these crops,
the strengthening of these cattle,
the plenteous harvest of these streams?

We do not walk the parish now,
the preacher says,
for walls and fences
and bricks and mortar
bar our way,
and the crops are gone

But yet,
as God's own people here,
we must give time,
and walk the parish bounds
in thought and prayer,
embrace the streets and alleyways
that are our harvest home.

And so we do:
with cross and banners lifted high
in song and celebration,
we ask the saints
of then and now
to intercede with God,
that harvests might be full.

And we, too,
play our part,
for when our Sunday worship
is complete,
and Communion is a holy memory,
we take our alms
of gifts and charity,
of work for justice and for peace,
into the harvest fields
that are our streets,
and homes,
and concrete darkness,
and wider broken world.

This is Rogation Day,
when saints and we,
all blessed by God,
will make the harvest come,
again,
in a very different harvest field,
as yet another year
unfolds.

Tom Gordon

Note: Rogation comes from the Latin 'rogo', meaning 'to ask'. Traditionally what is asked for, in England, on rogation days (the Monday, Tuesday and Wednesday before Ascension Day) is a blessing on the earth that it may produce a good harvest. Rogation days fell into disuse as people moved into urban areas and away from agricultural work. (New liturgies relating to rogation themes can be found in Cherish the Earth, *p. 179–198, Mary Low, Wild Goose Publications.)*

FIRE AND BREAD

God of Eastertide –
of blazing bonfires and familiar gestures,
of serious questions and tears and laughter,
of conversations on the road –

come close to us as we walk,
as we warm ourselves,
as we dance in firelight,
as we share stories and food.

Bless us as we celebrate your rising in us,
closer to us than breathing,
life-giving as fire and bread.

Ruth Burgess

THE BIBLE IN ABOUT
AN HOUR

THE BIBLE IN ABOUT AN HOUR

'The Bible in about an hour' is an attempt to do for the Bible what the 'Reduced Shake-speare Company' has done for Shakespeare – but, as the play needed to cover the period of time from the beginning of all things until now, it couldn't be reduced to much less than an hour! It is intended for performance in a church building, so there are very few stage directions as each church building will have its own possibilities and problems. Use the whole building if possible. The pace should not flag; there should be no pauses between the different 'scenes'. The mood is light, except for the section about the death of Jesus, where the slow drumbeat will help to achieve a contrast in mood. Casting can be very flexible. It is intended for a group of people who each take a number of parts; a change of a role signified by a simple change of a hat, or something similar where neces-sary. How the parts are shared out will depend on the number of actors you have avail-able. The only part that the same person must take throughout is that of the narrator.

Narrator:	So, to begin at the very beginning: 'In the beginning God created the heaven and the Earth ...' *(There is dramatic music and members of the cast come from different parts of the church carrying placards/pictures of the different parts of creation – sun, moon, water ... The narrator announces them as they arrive.)* He made ... *(Then, when all the placards/pictures are in place, the narrator announces:)* and people ... *(The man and woman enter, wearing the labels MAN/ADAM, WOMAN/EVE, and take their places alongside the rest of creation. The narrator strolls around the group.)* God looked at it all and decided it was good. He even created the idea of a good rest *(everyone flops to the ground)*. It was all lovely. *(Some peaceful music ... Then the woman gets up and begins wandering around.)*
Woman:	It's all so lovely ... *(The snake peeps out from behind a pillar, if the church has one.)*
Snake:	Pssst. Over here.
Woman:	Hello. Isn't it all lovely? So much to look at! So much to enjoy!
Snake:	Oh, you're so naive.
Woman:	What do you mean? Who are you anyway? Have we given you a name yet?
Snake:	Snake. At you service. All kinds of advice given. And you sure can use some advice!

Woman:	Advice? I don't think I need it. I have everything I need. God is so good to us!
Snake:	Good to you? Grow up, lady! Here, have an apple (*offering her an apple*). Wouldn't you like to eat this?
Woman:	Oh yes! Thank you. It's so lovely! But – wait – that's the tree God told us not to eat from.
Snake:	Quite. Just as I thought: Here you are in the middle of all this lovely fruit and you can't even touch it! What sort of a life is that?
Woman:	But that's the only fruit we can't eat. There are lots of other fruit. I don't really need that one.
Snake:	Don't need it! Who's saying anything about needing it? Don't you *want* it? Look how gorgeous it is. Smell it … Mmmm … Touch it …
Woman:	It *is* very nice.
Snake:	Nice! It's just what you've always wanted. Here. Eat it.
Woman:	But what would God say?
Snake:	Why should he say anything? You have a right to have what *you* want. You ought to eat it. Make your own decisions … Just try a little.
Woman:	Oh, since you put it like that. A little taste can't hurt, can it? (*She takes a bite.*) It's very tasty. I'll share it with Adam. (*She goes and does that.*)
Narrator:	So, things got in a mess early on in the story. (*There is a crack of thunder/a loud noise. The man and woman cower and cover their faces. Then, hand in hand, heads bowed down, they walk slowly away as the thunder/noise fades.*) … It wasn't all bad. There were people who really became God's friends and obeyed him – even when what he asked seemed ridiculous – like building a ship hundreds of miles from the sea. (*The cast join together to sing:*)

Noah's song

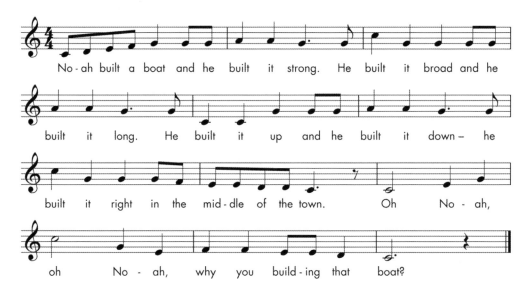

No-ah built a boat and he built it strong. He built it broad and he
built it long. He built it up and he built it down – he
built it right in the mid-dle of the town. Oh No - ah,
oh No - ah, why you build-ing that boat?

Noah told the people: 'It's going to rain
and life isn't ever going to be the same.'
But they said, 'Noah, see the sun does shine –
our present climate just suits us fine.'

Chorus

Noah and his wife and his sons' wives too,
and Shem, Ham and Japheth made up the crew.
They took on food and lots of drink.
And plenty of tar so the boat wouldn't sink.

Chorus

All the people watched and had a good laugh
when they saw Mrs Noah pushing on a giraffe.
And the word went round, 'Come and see the show,'
when Shem rode up on a buffalo.

Chorus

So at last the boat was as full as can be
and closely resembled a menagerie.
And Noah warned the people once again:
'Take care, for God's sending you lots of rain!'

Chorus

But the people mocked and the people scorned
and the people laughed when Noah warned.
So Noah shut the door on his great big boat
and waited to see if the thing would float.

Chorus

Then the skies grew dark and the thunder rolled;
and the wind blew hard and the air grew cold;
and the rain fell down and the flood swept through,
but Noah was safe with all his crew.

Chorus

So the days passed by and the sun came out;
and all Noah's family let out a shout:
'The rain's stopped raining, the ground is dry;
there's a great big rainbow in the sky.'
Oh Noah,
oh Noah,
we're glad you builded that boat.

Narrator: There were moments of real insight:

(Solo: 'The Lord is my Shepherd'/Psalm 23 sung/read)

And there were times when people – who should have known better really – messed
it up again and everything seemed to go wrong.

('By the waters of Babylon'/Psalm 137 sung/read by a group)

At length God decided the time had come to sort things out rather than to patch
them up. So one day, when Mary was –

Player: Mary?! Do you mean you've got to Mary?! Thousands of years in (*checks
watch*) _____ minutes!

Narrator: This is supposed to be a *brief* history! You can read up on it in your own
time. Here (*hands the player a large Bible. The player sits down and begins
to read.*)

Narrator: As I was saying, one day, when Mary was just pottering around the
house ...

Mary:	(*wearing an apron, carrying a feather duster*) I'll just finish this. Then I'd better go to the well and get some water. Maybe I'll see Joseph on the way. We need to see we've got all the wedding arrangements sorted.
Angel:	Hail! You who are highly favoured.
Mary:	Hello. Sorry, I didn't hear you knocking. I must have been miles away. *What* did you say?
Angel:	Hail! You who are highly favoured. God is with you. You are blessed among women.
Mary:	I think you must have the wrong house. Who were you looking for?
Angel:	Hail, Mary, you who are –
Mary:	Who are you? Do I know you?
Angel:	I am Gabriel.
Mary:	I can't think of anyone I know called Gabriel.
Angel:	The angel Gabriel
Mary:	Yes, I know there's an angel called Gabriel in the – you're *what*?!
Angel:	I am him ... he ... the angel Gabriel is me ... I've a message for you.
Mary:	Who from?
Angel:	God, of course. Do pay attention. You are to have a child.
Mary:	Oh yes. I hope Joseph and I will have many children.
Angel:	No, you are to have a child somewhat before that. In nine months to be precise.
Mary:	What! But ...
Angel:	A special child. The Messiah. The Promised One. The Saviour of the world.
Mary:	But ... me ... but ... it's not possible.
Angel:	Remember that with God anything is possible.
Mary:	(*after a long pause*) Then, let it be as God wishes. But ... *me?* ...

(*Optional song: 'The angel Gabriel from heaven came' or 'Ave Maria'*)

Mary:	But what will people say? How am I ever going to explain this to Joseph? How am I ever going to explain this to mum and dad? People have been hoping for the Messiah for hundreds of years ... How am I going to manage? God, you're going to have to really help me!
Player:	(*looking up from Bible*) Right – then there was Christmas – everybody knows that bit – but what happens next? How did she manage? How did Joseph cope? How did people react to having the Messiah living next door? That's what I want to know.
Narrator:	All right, one story – that's all we've got time for.
Mary:	(*sets off down the aisle with a few other women*) It's been a really good week, hasn't it? It's not often that we get to Jerusalem.
Woman:	It's been such a treat to see Jesus with you this year. Nearly time for his bar mitzvah now, isn't it? Don't they grow up quickly? Where is he by the way?
Mary:	Oh, he thinks he's one of the men now, even though he's only twelve. He'll be with Joseph and his friends. (*Joseph sets off down the aisle with some of the men.*)
Man:	So have you got much work to go back to, Joseph?
Joseph:	Enough to keep me busy. Mustn't grumble.
Man:	I expect that boy of yours will be a big help to you now. He's growing up fast. Must nearly be time for his bar mitzvah. Where is he by the way?
Joseph:	Oh, he may think he's grown up, but he's still one of the children. He'll be with Mary.
Mary and Joseph:	(*together, to each other*) Where is he? Isn't he with you? No, he's not with me. Isn't he with you? (*They rush up the aisle and grab Jesus.*)
Joseph:	Where have you been? What do you think you're playing at? Don't you realise your mother's been off her head with worry?
Jesus:	(*very politely*) But didn't you realise I'd be in the Temple, my Father's house?
Player:	So what happened then?
Narrator:	Well, they just seem to have gone back home to Nazareth and got on with life. It couldn't have been easy. But at least it was only the family

that knew there was anything different about Jesus – and a few shepherds – and an innkeeper and his wife, but they lived right at the other
end of the country. And they didn't have the media to worry about in
those days. Not that that made any difference once he got going when
he was about thirty. Then everybody was talking about him. *(A gossiping
group forms.)*

Gossip 1:   Have you heard what Jesus has been saying? There was this big crowd of
people on the side of the mountain – and do you know what he said?

Jesus: You have heard it said: 'An eye for an eye and a tooth for a tooth.' But I
say, if anyone hits you on the right cheek, turn the other cheek to him
too. *(Two players mime this in slapstick-style – laughter.)* You have heard it
said: 'Love your neighbour and hate your enemy' *(the player who was
'hit' turns on the attacker).* But I tell you to love your enemies and pray
for them and do good to them. *(The players hug.)* Don't judge people.
Listen.

Player 2:   *(holding a log of wood in front of his face and groping his way)* Tut tut. Did
you know you have a speck of dust in your eye? You should really be
more careful.

Player 3:   Gerroff! How can you see with that whacking great log in *your* eye?
Leave me alone.

Player 2:   Don't be silly – I can see your speck quite clearly.

Jesus: You hypocrite! First get rid of the log out of your own eye, and then you
may be able to see what is in your friend's eye ... Do you remember the
two men in the village by the sea who built new houses last year?

Man 2:   So how's the building going?

Man 3:   Very well. Nearly finished. I'll be moving in next week.

Man 2:   Gosh, how have you managed that? I've barely got beyond the founda-
tions. You want to be careful about those cowboy builders.

Man 3:   Well, if you will choose to build on solid rock, what can you expect? It
must be costing you a packet! Now, my plot is on the plain by the sea.
Nice soft soil. Easy to excavate. No problem. Come and use my spare
room if you need to move before your new house is finished.

*(Song: 'The wise man built his house upon the rock', sung by a group of children, if possi-
ble. Man 2 and Man 3 mime the song.)*

Gossip 1:	And then he said that listening to his words was like building upon the rock – hard work sometimes but the only thing to do really.
Gossip 2:	I don't know what to make of him. He's offended a lot of people. I mean – who does he think he is?
Gossip 1:	He tells really good stories though. Have you heard the one about the two sons? Just like that family down the road from me.
Son:	Dad.
Father:	Yes, son.
Son:	Dad ...
Father:	Yes, son.
Son:	*(making an enormous effort to get it out)* I want my money.
Father:	Your money? And what money would that be then?
Son:	I want the money that's coming to me when you ... well ... when you're not here any more. And I want it now.
Father:	Why's that son?
Son:	Never mind why. It's time I had some fun. I want it now. It's mine. I want my rights.
Father:	Very well, son
Son:	Eh?
Father:	Here it is. Be careful what you do with it. God go with you.
Son:	Forget all that stuff ... Ha, I didn't think it was going to be that easy! Now I can get away from this place and have some fun. *(He strolls away and is joined by a partying crowd. They make a loud 'we're enjoying ourselves' sort of noise.)* This is the life: wine, women and song. And more wine, and more women, and lots of really good friends. When I think of all those years I wasted. Barman, another round for my friends.
Barman:	Sorry, mate. Not till you've paid your bills for all this lot.
Son:	*(turning his pockets inside out)* Who's going to lend me something then?
Mate:	Not till you've paid back my last loan.

Others:	And mine ... And mine ... *(They all turn away from him.)*
Son:	No problem. I'll get a job to tide me over. I'll just pop down to the Job Centre. No problem.
Job Centre employee:	So, what was your last job?
Son:	Well ... I used to help out on my dad's farm – sometimes ...
Job Centre employee:	So what happened?
Son:	I left ...
Job Centre employee:	So, not made redundant. Have you any references?
Son:	Well, no.
Job Centre employee:	No references ... Well, the only thing I can offer you is this vacancy on Mr Eli's farm. Not a great wage I'm afraid. But then, you have no references. He needs an extra hand in the pig breeding section.
Son:	Pigs! But, I'm a Jew. I don't have anything to do with pigs!
Job Centre employee:	Sorry. That's all there is. Goodbye. Have a nice day.
Son:	Pigs! I'm so hungry I could even fancy some of this pig feed. Ugh! Maybe not quite. God, what am I going to do? The pay is so low I'll never pay back my debts. And I haven't even had any pay yet! The most hopeless worker on dad's farm was treated better than this. That's it! I'll go and ask him for a job. Anything would be better than this. *(He sets off round the church to the music of the Spiritual 'Going home'. His dad rushes to meet him.)*
Son:	Dad. I don't think you'll want me for a son any more. I've really messed things up. But could you let me have a job please? I'll do anything, I'll –
Father:	It's so good to have you back. Hey, everybody! He's back! My son that went away – he's back! I thought he was dead. Bring him some clean clothes someone. Get the champagne out. Ask the neighbours round. Let's have a party.
Son 2:	What's going on?

Father:	Your brother's back! Isn't it wonderful?
Son 2:	Just like that! He's back – so you roll out the red carpet and kill the fatted calf. What about me? What about all the work I've done since he left? How can you just forgive him like that?
Father:	Son, you know I love you. Everything I have is yours. Don't be jealous because I am so happy.
Gossip 1:	Aww, isn't that lovely? ... I wonder what happened next?
Gossip 2:	Haven't you heard what he's been doing? I don't know what to make of it. Mixing with the likes of that Mary from Magdala – not to mention people like tax collectors. And ... he's going about healing people.
Gossip 1:	No ... Does he really? What sort of people?
Gossip 2:	Blind, lame, deaf, paralysed ... You name it. There was this crowd of over 5,000 the other day, just listening and being healed and things ... He had them eating out of his hand.
Disciple 1:	My insides tell me it's time to finish now, Jesus. Teatime.
Disciple 2:	And if we're not careful, they'll be expecting us to *provide* tea.
Jesus:	Good idea. We'll do that. Correction: You'll do that.
Disciple 1:	Don't be daft! Where are we supposed to get that amount of food from? Any amount of food from, come to that! You may not have noticed but we're not exactly convenient for the Cash and Carry!
Jesus:	Anybody got any food?

(A child comes and offers a picnic box. Jesus takes some rolls from it and carefully puts them in baskets, which already contain lots of pieces of bread hidden under cloths. He gives the baskets of bread to the disciples. With expressions of amazement, the disciples give each person in the audience a piece of bread.)

Gossip 1: You mean he fed them all with that little boy's picnic? Now that's what I call a miracle! Who *is* he, do you think?

Gossip 2: Well, some people are wondering if he is the Messiah ... *(Music, while the cast run down to the door of the church. They begin a procession around the church, making their way to the front. As they process they lay coats, scarves, etc in front of Jesus.*

They have armfuls of branches which they wave and give to people in the audience. They sing (with the audience joining in on the chorus):

Hosanna

Ho - san - na, ho - san - na,   shout hoo - ray,   wel - come the King

rid - ing   on   a   bor - rowed don - key;   all the peo - ple sing   and   shout,

spread their coats to form   a   car - pet,   wave green bran - ches all   a - bout.

Can this man be   our   Mes - si - ah?   Has he come to   set   us   free?

Can he   be   the one who's com - ing   to bring hope for you   and   me?

Chorus

2. Is he coming to the city
    to seize power and take control?
    Is he out for domination?
    World authority his goal?

Chorus

3. Let's all join and shout Hosanna
    just in case it all comes true.
    Just in case he really is the
    one who's King of me and you.

Chorus

(There's a great shout of Hooray! as the procession reaches the front of the church. Then a slow drumbeat begins. The players run to different parts of the church. The lights dim and there is a spotlight on the narrator. The narrator speaks from the front; the rest of the cast speak from different points around the church.)

Narrator:	Jesus ate the Passover meal with his friends. He took some of the bread and said: 'This is my body.' And he passed around the cup of wine and told them all to drink it, saying: 'This is my blood.'
A:	What does he mean?
B:	What is he talking about?
C:	What's the matter, Jesus? The Passover is supposed to be fun!
Jesus:	One of you is going to betray me.
D:	What does he mean?
E:	What's he talking about?
F:	Surely you don't mean one of us?
G:	Surely you don't mean me?
Narrator:	Judas went out. And it was night. In that night Judas betrayed him. Jesus was arrested and put on trial. Most of the disciples ran away.
Peter:	But I haven't. I'm here.
Onlooker 1:	Aren't you one of his friends?
Peter:	No!
Onlooker 2:	Haven't I seen you with him?
Peter:	No! No!
Onlooker 3:	I think you're one of his followers.
Peter:	No! No! No!
Narrator:	Jesus turned and caught Peter's eye. And Peter went away and wept. The night dragged on. The trial ended. The verdict was given.
Many voices:	Crucify him!
Narrator:	So he was crucified. *(The spotlight moves to the cross. The drumbeat gets gradually slower – and suddenly stops. There's a moment of silence. Then there is a roll of drums. The players rush up to the front of the church.)*
A:	I've seen him!

B:	He's alive!
C:	I touched him!
D:	He's alive!
E:	How can it have happened?
F:	He's alive!

(One of the group grabs a microphone and becomes a TV interviewer. Another grabs clapperboards and calls out: 'Camera! Action!')

Interviewer:	Something very strange has happened in Jerusalem today. There are reports that Jesus of Nazareth, the preacher who was executed for unspecified crimes against the state on Friday afternoon, has been seen walking around – fit and well. The story is unconfirmed as yet. But the city is full of rumours. (*The cast wander round the church whispering to the audience: 'He's alive.'*)
Narrator:	Jesus said to them: 'Go out to all the world. Go and tell everyone about me.' (*One of the cast takes a tall cross and walks over to other members of the cast.*)
1:	(*with cross*) Hello.
2:	Who are you?
3:	I haven't seen you here before.
4:	Where have you come from?
5:	What have you come for?
1:	I've come to tell you about someone called Jesus.
2:	Never heard of him.
3:	Where does he live?
4:	Who is he?
5:	What's he got to do with us?
1:	He has everything to do with you here in _____ (*village/town/city*).

2:   OK! Hour's up! Let's go for it! (*The cast strike attitudes around the narra-tor and then declaim the following together, or individuals could read out four lines each:*)

Genesis, Exodus, Leviticus, Numbers,
Deuteronomy, Joshua, Judges and Ruth,
One and two Samuel, Kings and Chronicles,
Ezra, Nehemiah and Esther forsooth,
patient Job and Psalms and Proverbs,
Ecclesiastes and Solomon's song,
seventeen books of seventeen prophets,
that's the Old Testament. Now move on
a few hundred years and we're in the New Testament,
Gospels four, Matthew, Mark, Luke and John,
Acts of the Apostles, lots of letters
sent by the apostles to help the church on;
then there's Revelation, full of visions
strange and mysterious – things that are yet to be.
All in the Bible, read all about it.
Our play has ended. Come and have tea!

Margaret Harvey

SONGS AND PRAYERS
FOR THE JOURNEY

IN THE KINGDOM'S VENTURES

Words and music: Ian M. Fraser

A - men, a - men, a - men, a - men. A - men, a - men.

Now we go to live out
all we promised:
let our words and deeds say
'Yes! Amen!'

Glory to the Father
and to Jesus,
to the Holy Spirit,
Three in One.

As in the beginning,
now and ever,
to the end of ages
'Yes! Amen!'

Note: The extended amens come only at the end of the fourth verse.

BEYOND EASTER

Beyond Easter
we go singing

Having been grabbed
by resurrection
we are full of tears and laughter.

The way ahead is unknown.
It will always be like that.

But having danced in the light
we will look for glory everywhere.

Ruth Burgess

GOD OF THE ELEMENTS

God of the elements
bless us with resurrection.

Burn away in us
what needs to go.

Wash us clean
and clear and holy.

Blow us round
with warmth and wonder.

Root us deeply each day
in love and justice.

God of the elements
bless us with resurrection.

Ruth Burgess

IN YOU I LOVE AND GLORY

I will put my hand
in your hand
because
I trust you.

I will live my life
your way:
through hope
and through justice.

Whatever heaven is
I will go there
with you.

You are my birth
my life
my death
and my resurrection.

In you,
O God,
I love
and glory.

Ruth Burgess

SWEET JESUS

Sweet Jesus,
you know;

you know
our loves
our hurts
our desolation;

you know
our joy
in you
and in each other;

you know
our fear
of death
and of painful dying.

Sweet Jesus,
after Easter,
we know
that you know,

and we are full of hope
and wonder.

Ruth Burgess

LEAD US AND BLESS US

God our Maker,
Star-giver,
warm us.

God in Jesus,
storyteller,
call us.

God the Holy Spirit,
traveller,
caress us.

God of all our nights and days
lead us
and bless us.

Ruth Burgess

RISEN LORD

(A heart for the simple things)

Words and music: da Noust

Ris - en Lord, give us a heart for the sim - ple things: love, laugh - ter, bread and wine and dreams. Give us a green_____ and grow - ing hope. And make of us a peo - ple whose song is 'al - le - lu - ia'. Whose name is love, whose sign is peace.

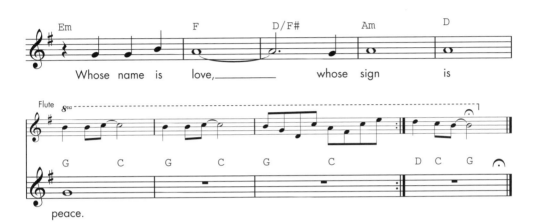

Whose name is love,_____ whose sign is

peace.

SOURCES AND ACKNOWLEDGEMENTS

Every effort has been made to trace copyright holders of all the items reproduced in this book. We would be glad to hear from anyone whom we have been unable to contact so that any omissions can be rectified in future editions.

'Looking in the wrong places' – by Kathy Galloway, from *Talking to the Bones*, Kathy Galloway, SPCK, 1996. Used by permission of Kathy Galloway and SPCK.

'Easter '78' – by Ruth Burgess, from *At Ground Level*, Wild Goose Publications, out of print.

'Peter and Mary' – by Jan Sutch Pickard, from *Imaginary Conversations: Dialogues for use in worship and Bible study*, The Methodist Overseas Division, 1989/90. Used by permission of Jan Sutch Pickard.

'Two friends' – by Jan Sutch Pickard, from *Imaginary Conversations: Dialogues for use in worship and Bible study*, The Methodist Overseas Division, 1989/90. Used by permission of Jan Sutch Pickard.

'Enemy of Apathy' – by John L. Bell and Graham Maule, from *Enemy of Apathy : Sixty-two songs and chants for Lent, Eastertide and Pentecost*, Wild Goose Publications, © Wild Goose Resource Group. Used by permission of the Wild Goose Resource Group.

'On everyone who looks to God' – words by Ian Masson Fraser; music (Enabling Spirit) by Ian Masson Fraser, arranged by Douglas Galbraith. Words and music copyright Stainer & Bell Ltd, 23 Gruneisen Road, London N3 1DZ, UK. www.stainer.co.uk

'Lord God, whose Spirit drives us out' – words by Ian Masson Fraser. Words copyright Stainer & Bell Ltd, 23 Gruneisen Road, London N3 1DZ, UK. www.stainer.co.uk

'All is well' – Music, English traditional ('Poor bird'), author of words unknown. From *Forward to the Promised Community Worship Book*, Churches Together in Britain and Ireland (CTBI), 1998. Used by permission of CTBI.

'Their earthly journey closed' – words by Ian Masson Fraser; music (GFM) by Donald Rennie. Words and music copyright Stainer & Bell Ltd, 23 Gruneisen Road, London N3 1DZ, UK. www.stainer.co.uk

'Audaciously and graciously' – words by Ian Masson Fraser; music (Delight in Bodily Life) by Ian Masson Fraser, arranged by Duncan Anderson. Words and Music Copyright Stainer & Bell Ltd, 23 Gruneisen Road, London N3 1DZ, UK. www.stainer.co.uk

'Knowing her blessing' – by Chris Polhill, first published in *A Book of Blessings: and how to write your* own, Wild Goose Publications, 2001. Used by permission of Chris Polhill.

'Great Spirit, give us hearts to understand ...' – as found in the United Nations Environmental Sabbath kit of April 1988.

'Getting the wean done' – Erik Cramb, from *Parables and Patter*, Wild Goose Publications, out of print.

'Shot through and through with wonder' – words by Ian Masson Fraser; music (New Life) by Ian Masson Fraser, arranged by Donald Rennie. Words and music copyright Stainer & Bell Ltd, 23 Gruneisen Road, London N3 1DZ, UK. www.stainer.co.uk

'See it is done' – words by Ian Masson Fraser. Words © Stainer & Bell Ltd, 23 Gruneisen Road, London N3 1DZ. www.stainer.co.uk

'Doubt and faith' – words by Ian Masson Fraser. Words © Stainer & Bell Ltd, 23 Gruneisen Road, London N3 1DZ. www.stainer.co.uk

'Not just to prayer and worship we're committed' – words by Ian Masson Fraser; music (Church Militant) by Donald Rennie. Words and Music copyright Stainer & Bell Ltd, 23 Gruneisen Road, London N3 1DZ, UK. www.stainer.co.uk

'Grapes' – Ruth Burgess, from *At Ground Level*, Wild Goose Publications, out of print.

'This door?' – by Tom Gordon, from *New Journeys Now Begin: Learning on the path of grief and loss*, Wild Goose Publications, 2006.

'Feast of life' – Voices at the beginning of this liturgy from stories told to Neil Paynter: Voice 2: Alan Hawkins, Voice 3: Helen O'Donnell, Voice 4: Camilla Björkborn.

'Bread' – words © Pat Bennett; tune (Nafziger) and arrangement © John L. Bell. Tune and arrangement originally from the song 'I owe my Lord a morning song', *I Will Not Sing Alone*, John L. Bell & Graham Maule, Wild Goose Publications, 2002. Tune and arrangement used by permission of the Wild Goose Resource Group.

'We're longing for a different world' – words by Ian Masson Fraser; music (Justice is the Key) by Ian Masson Fraser, arranged by Donald Rennie. Words and music © Stainer & Bell Ltd, 23 Gruneisen Road, London N3 1DZ. www.stainer.co.uk

'And are the bread and wine your body, Lord?' – words by Ian Masson Fraser. Words © Stainer & Bell Ltd, 23 Gruneisen Road, London N3 1DZ. www.stainer.co.uk

'At the gates' – by Jan Sutch Pickard, from *Out of Iona: Words from a crossroads of the world*, Wild Goose Publications, 2003. Used by permission of Jan Sutch Pickard.

'At the gates' is from the sequence 'Faslane 2002'.

'Glory to God in the High Street' – words by Ian Masson Fraser; music (Venturing) by Ian Masson Fraser, arranged by Donald Rennie. Words and music © Stainer & Bell Ltd, 23 Gruneisen Road, London N3 1DZ. www.stainer.co.uk

'Hymn of thanksgiving for lambing' – This music arrangement © 1991 Kevin Mayhew Ltd., reproduced by permission. Kevin Mayhew Ltd, Buxhall, Stowmarket, IP14 3BW, UK. www.kevinmayhewltd.com

'In the Kingdom's ventures' – words by Ian Masson Fraser; music (Benediction/variation on original tune) by Ian Masson Fraser. Words and music © 1974 Stainer & Bell Ltd, 23 Gruneisen Road, London N3 1DZ. www.stainer.co.uk

CONTRIBUTORS

Rowena Aberdeen-de Voil is currently the MacLeod Centre warden. She is passionate about community in all its forms and enjoys diversity and creativity in life and worship.

Stuart Barrie is a retired engineer living in East Kilbride.

Elizabeth Baxter enjoys writing liturgy and poetry and accompanying people on their life journeys at Holy Rood House in Thirsk and Hexthorpe Manor in Doncaster. She finds inspiration and fun in community and family life.

John L. Bell – With his colleagues, John has produced collections of original songs, compilations of music from the World Church, and books of worship resources and sermons. He works throughout Europe, North America, Australia and New Zealand for churches of all denominations. In 1999 he was honoured by the Presbyterian Church of Canada and the Royal School of Church Music, which bestowed a Fellowship on him; in 2002, he was awarded an honorary doctorate by the University of Glasgow. He is an occasional broadcaster on BBC radio and television.

Pat Bennett is a PhD student, researching in the area of spirituality and health. She is an associate member of the Iona Community and has been writing prayers, liturgies, meditations, hymns and songs since her first stay on Iona in 1996.

Jan Berry lives with her partner in Manchester, is a minister in the United Reformed Church, and teaches practical theology at Luther King House. She has a passionate interest in feminist liturgy and ritual, and enjoys creating material for worship.

Ruth Bowen is a Friend of the Iona Community. She divides her time between her home, family and work as a learning support teacher in Clevedon, Somerset, and her island home on Stronsay, Orkney. She loves the islands, woolcraft, gardening and people. She believes in the ministry of prayer, healing and reconciliation.

Ted Bowman is an educator, trainer and writer. His primary work is about grief and loss and the stories created about losses.

Alix Brown is a member of the Iona Community.

Julia Brown works in Durham where she lives with her husband and three children. Writing poetry is one of the ways in which she is exploring her latent creativity.

Nick Burden lives in Newcastle upon Tyne and worships at St Gabriel's Church, Heaton. He is an associate of the Iona Community.

Ruth Burgess lives in Sunderland with a large and hungry black and white cat. She works with people with dementia and is also an editor and a writer. She likes the sea and fireworks and growing things to enjoy and eat.

Beryl Chatfield is a retired teacher and United Reformed Church minister. She is interested in people, world development issues and interfaith dialogue.

David Coleman is a member of the Iona Community.

Ian Cowie came to the Iona Community on leaving the hospital and army back in 1945. He was the first Iona Abbey guide, then served as a minister in three parishes and finally as chaplain to the Christian Fellowship of Healing. He published five books: *Growing Knowing Jesus, People Praying, Across the Spectrum, Prayers and Ideas for Healing Services* (Wild Goose Publications), and *Jesus' Healing Works and Ours* (Wild Goose Publications). Ian died in 2005 at age 81.

Erik Cramb maintains that the critical formation of his ministry took place in Glasgow's Gallowgate and shaped his later ministry as an industrial chaplain. 'Theology on the hoof' is the chaplain's stock-in-trade, responding to the insights, longings and wisdom of those who would never think of darkening the church's door, except perhaps for a funeral, or wedding or a 'christening'. His seminary for theology on the hoof was the tenements, shops, pubs and street corners of the East End of his native city.

Judy Dinnen – 'It was on a creative week in Iona years ago that I first discovered creative writing. Since then I've written poems, studied and led workshops in schools and community. Writing as a way of exploring faith plays a part in my life as a curate in South Herefordshire.'

Carol Dixon lives in Northumberland where she is a lay preacher in the United Reformed Church. She is a member of the Companions of Brother Lawrence, an ecumenical prayer fellowship, and a Friend of St Cuthbert's, Holy Island, and her hymns have been published in *All year round, Songs for the New Millennium, Worship Live* and the new Church of Scotland Hymnary. She is married with a daughter and twin sons and enjoys being a grandmother.

Carol Dougall came to work at the Abbey in 1988 on a three-year contract. However, she married an islander and now lives on Iona permanently. Having experienced an average of fifteen power cuts a year, she's become a little obsessed!

Leith Fisher has recently retired after ministries in Falkirk, Glasgow Calton and Wellington. Leith is a hymn writer and the author of *Will you follow me?: Exploring the Gospel of Mark* and *The Widening Road – from Bethlehem to Emmaus: An Exploration of the Gospel of Luke* (Scottish Christian Press). He is married to Nonie and they have five grown-up children. Leith has been a member of the Iona Community since 1966.

Andrew Foster is an engineer living in Ontario, Canada, a Friend of the Iona Community, an elder in The Presbyterian Church in Canada, a frequent visitor to Iona, and a contributor to some of Ruth Burgess's previous books.

David Fox was born in Newbridge, Monmouthshire. He studied chemistry in University College London and taught for a while in Reading. Now a minister of the United Reformed Church serving in Penarth, he has contributed to a number of ecumenical publications for CTBI and Cytûn and has had hymns published in a number of collections both at home and overseas.

Ian M. Fraser – 'The main thing about my life is that Margaret married me, I have three children, nine grandchildren and two great-grandchildren.' Ian became a member of the Iona Community in 1941. He is the author of many books, recently *The Way Ahead: Grown-up Christians* (Wild Goose Publications).

Alma Fritchley is fairly new to faith and is a member of the Metropolitan Community Church. She is a civil servant and a published novelist whose love of whodunnits has inspired her. She lives with her civil partner in Manchester.

Kathy Galloway is the current leader of the Iona Community.

Douglas Galbraith is the Ecumenical Officer of the Church of Scotland and Precentor of its General Assembly. He is a member of the Iona Community.

Terry Garley is the Ecumenical Development Officer for Churches Together in Lancashire, before which she was County Ecumenical Officer from 1990–2000 in Derbyshire and Nottinghamshire. The Anglican partner in an Anglican–Methodist marriage, she served on the group which produced an Anglican–Methodist Covenant signed on 1 November, 2003 in the presence of Her Majesty the Queen. During the 1990s, Terry was Deputy Moderator of the Churches Together in England Forum (1990–1995) and Moderator (1995–1999).

Liz Gibson lives in Oban with her husband, Martyn, and their two sons, Paul and Hamish. She is a Church of Scotland minister and a hospital chaplain. She enjoys developing new ideas for worship in conjunction with the church's worship group. She became a member of the Iona Community in 1998, and has been involved with the community's centres on Iona and at Camas on the isle of Mull.

Tom Gordon is a member of the Iona Community. He is the author of two books, *A Need for Living* (Wild Goose Publications) and *New Journeys Now Begin* (Wild Goose Publications), which explore end of life and bereavement issues. He is also a frequent contributor to various anthologies. He has been a hospice chaplain since 1994.

Liz Gregory-Smith lives with her husband in New Brancepeth, near Durham. They have two adult sons. Liz is a Reader at the local Anglican church. She enjoys creative writing and writing people's memories.

David Hamflett is a Methodist minister and a Friend of the Iona Community, working in the north of England. He has a special interest in compiling and composing liturgies. He also particularly enjoys playing and singing traditional folk songs and tunes.

Sheila Hamil is a priest in the Church of England, retired from parish work in the North-East of England, but still keen to do outreach work and evangelism projects wherever God leads. She is also a Christian singer/songwriter, and a drama and assembly scriptwriter. Much of her work can be obtained through her website www.sheilahamil.co.uk

Mary Hanrahan is an active member of St Paul's Parish (RC), Shettleston and is a primary school teacher. She enjoys reading and writing poetry and has been published in various small press magazines.

John Harvey is a member of the Iona Community.

Margaret Harvey is a founder member of the Coleg y Groes Community and helps to run Coleg y Groes Retreat House in Corwen, North Wales. www.colegygroes.co.uk She is a native of Wales and a Church in Wales priest.

Ruth Harvey is the editor of *Coracle*, the magazine of the Iona Community, and a part-time university chaplain in Carlisle. She lives in Cumbria with Nick and their three girls.

David Hawkey is an associate member of the Iona Community and is married to Frances. A science technology teacher by trade, he is always learning from children and sharing the deep magic of creation. He was the Sacristan on Iona in 2000. He is now involved with the International Centre for Reconciliation at Coventry Cathedral.

Frances Hawkey is an associate of the Iona Community, married to David and with four adult daughters and nine grandchildren. After living in a flat for ten years in the inner city council estate where she and David worked, she worked as the Iona Abbey housekeeper for a year. She now lives in multicultural Coventry and is involved in 'building bridges'. She draws her writing inspiration largely from the places where she has lived and worked.

Paul Heppleston is a musician and writer currently based in Derbyshire. In his early retirement from research and teaching, he leads journeys with his wife, Hazel, to remote parts of Britain with Pilgrim Adventure www.pilgrim-adventure.org.uk

Judith Jessop is a Methodist minister currently working in Sheffield and a single parent caring for her two children. She is interested in new ways of thinking about and shaping Christian faith and would like to pursue issues of justice and peace. She hopes to become an associate member of the Iona Community.

Liz Knowles is a teacher and a Church of England Reader. She is married to Brian Chave.

Anne Lawson is vicar of Haslington and Crewe Green in Cheshire. She writes poetry in her spare time, often using the paradoxes which poetry allows to work out her theology.

David Lemmon is a recently retired youth worker and youth work trainer, living in Beckenham, Kent. He is a Methodist Local Preacher and a Friend of the Iona Community.

John McLuckie is a priest of the Scottish Episcopal Church and is part of the clergy team at Old St Paul's Church in Edinburgh. After working in parishes and in college chaplaincy, he has had a number of roles in the public sector and now works for the Scottish Public Services Ombudsman.

Rosie Miles rediscovered her poetic voice after a stay on Iona in 1999. 'Vision' was actually started while sitting on Staffa! Since then she has contributed to a number of Wild Goose anthologies, and most recently co-edited *Doing December Differently: An Alternative Christmas Handbook* (Wild Goose Publications, 2006) with Nicola Slee.

Peter Millar is the author of several books, including *Waymarks: Signposts to Discovering God's Presence in the World* (Canterbury Press) and *Our Hearts Still Sing: Daily Readings* (Wild Goose Publications). He is a member of the Iona Community.

Margaret Moakes continues to expand her creativity as a writer, alongside associate membership of a religious community, lay ministry in an ecumenical church and exploration of what God means in our complex 21st-century world.

Yvonne Morland is a member of the Iona Community.

da Noust are part of the ecumenical L'Arche Edinburgh community that welcomes people with learning disabilities, employed assistants and volunteers to a shared life founded on the values of simplicity, mutual faithfulness and accountability (www.larche.org.uk). Further community resources for shared prayer – songs, carols, texts – can be accessed via da_noust@yahoo.co.uk

Sarah Pascoe worked as a nurse. She is now a grandmother and lives in Tyneside.

Elizabeth Paterson, a member of the Iona Community, gardens organically, makes wonderful compost and gained an interest in natural medicine while working in Southern Sudan.

Neil Paynter has been an English teacher to immigrants to Canada, a nurse's aide, a 'counsellor', a night shelter worker, a mental health worker, a community worker, a farm labourer, a fruit picker, a security guard (reluctantly), a bookseller, a hospital cleaner, a stand-up comedian, a musician and an editorial assistant. He is an employee and an associate of the Iona Community. His books include *This is The Day: Readings and Meditations from the Iona Community* and *Lent & Easter Readings from Iona* (Wild Goose Publications) www.ionabooks.com

Jan Sutch Pickard, a writer and storyteller, lives on Mull, having worked for nearly six years in the Macleod Centre and Abbey on Iona. The pieces included here, however, were written when she lived in the heart of a city, or left Iona 'looking for peace and justice' to demonstrate against Trident.

Chris Polhill is the author of *A Pilgrim's Guide to Iona Abbey* and co-editor of *Eggs and Ashes: Practical and Liturgical Resources for Lent and Holy Week.* She is a member of the Iona Community.

Timothy Redman, a 'Geordie' from Newcastle, trained at the Manchester School of Music. He worked at the BBC for many years and held a number of appointments in churches as Director of Music. During the 1990s he was Director at Wellington Church, Glasgow. He was a gifted performer, arranger and composer with choir and organ. He died in 2005.

Donald Rennie is a member of the Iona Community.

Richard Sharples is a Methodist minister who served as the Warden of Iona Abbey from 2004 to 2007. He delights in walking, cycling and gardening and in a simple lifestyle. He is married to Biddy, with three daughters Annie, Mary and Eve.

Thom M. Shuman is a poet and a Presbyterian minister in Cincinnati, Ohio. He is the author of *The Jesse Tree* (Wild Goose Publications). Thom blogs at www.occasionalsightings.blogspot.com

Rachel Starr is a doctoral candidate at ISEDET, Buenos Aires, researching feminist theology, women and violence. She is blogging about her experience in Latin America http://earthandstarrs.blogspot.com

Zam Walker is a member of the Iona Community

Wellspring was born in 1998 when Catherine McElhinney and Kathryn Turner began making resources, used in parishes and schools, available to the wider world, particularly through their website. Now 1000 pages, the website is used by people all around the world – especially in poorer countries where online access opens up a wealth of affordable materials. www.wellsprings.org.uk

Unfortunately it was not possible to obtain biographical details of every contributor.

INDEX OF AUTHORS

Rowena Aberdeen-de Voil 246
Duncan Anderson 204

Stuart Barrie 237
Elizabeth Baxter 161, 170, 280
John L. Bell 162
Pat Bennett 25, 65, 69, 86, 206, 212, 233, 240, 248, 274
Jan Berry 21, 43, 52, 312
Ruth Bowen 115
Ted Bowman 244
Alix Brown 154
Julia Brown 62, 67, 314
Marion Brown 266
Nick Burden 96
Ruth Burgess 20, 32, 52, 74, 81, 105, 138, 140, 148, 164, 195, 198, 200, 226, 250, 255, 284, 320, 339, 340, 341

Beryl Chatfield 281
David Coleman 188
Churchill Community College students 65
Ian Cowie 262, 263, 264
Erik Cramb 222

da Noust 44, 48, 72, 254, 258, 300, 304, 306, 342
Lisa Debney 83
Simon de Voil 310
Judy Dinnen 61, 256
Carol Dixon 31, 112, 156, 158, 214, 218, 266
Carol Dougall 295

Leith Fisher 20, 90, 97, 166, 174, 193, 224, 243
Andrew Foster 77
David Fox 170
Ian M. Fraser 168, 176, 196, 204, 225, 236, 242, 245, 276, 279, 286, 338
Alma Fritchley 169, 171

Douglas Galbraith 168
Kathy Galloway 32
Terry Garley 94
Liz Gibson 218
Tom Gordon 103, 180, 226, 228, 240, 260, 277, 318

Liz Gregory-Smith 74, 76

David Hamflett 23, 142, 144, 148, 165, 192, 257
Sheila Hamil 63
Mary Hanrahan 80
John Harvey 40, 41, 141, 152, 202, 247, 287
Margaret Harvey 111, 179, 260, 313, 322
Ruth Harvey 162
David Hawkey 310
Frances Hawkey 176, 207, 282, 311, 315, 316
G.F. Handel 31
Paul Heppleston 295

Judith Jessop 67, 76, 78, 251, 272

Liz Knowles 158, 314, 316

Anne Lawson 175, 232
David Lemmon 70, 155

John McLuckie 161
Graham Maule 162
Rosie Miles 288
Peter Millar 66
Margaret Moakes 82
Yvonne Morland 108

Sarah Pascoe 24
Elizabeth Paterson 215, 216, 217
Neil Paynter 60, 189, 266, 289, 296, 300
Jan Sutch Pickard 87, 90, 281
Chris Polhill 68, 78, 106, 194, 209, 211, 216

Timothy Redman 97, 193
Donald Rennie 196, 225, 245, 276, 286
Paul Richardson 296

Richard Sharples 61, 92
Thom M. Shuman 26, 49, 73, 114, 146, 149, 157, 165, 178, 205, 223, 238, 250, 299, 317
Sandy Small 97, 193
Rachel Starr 273

Zam Walker 181, 185
Wellspring 172

THE IONA COMMUNITY IS:

- An ecumenical movement of men and women from different walks of life and different traditions in the Christian church
- Committed to the gospel of Jesus Christ, and to following where that leads, even into the unknown
- Engaged together, and with people of goodwill across the world, in acting, reflecting and praying for justice, peace and the integrity of creation
- Convinced that the inclusive community we seek must be embodied in the community we practise

Together with our staff, we are responsible for:

- Our islands residential centres of Iona Abbey, the MacLeod Centre on Iona, and Camas Adventure Centre on the Ross of Mull

and in Glasgow:

- The administration of the Community
- Our work with young people
- Our publishing house, Wild Goose Publications
- Our association in the revitalising of worship with the Wild Goose Resource Group

The Iona Community was founded in Glasgow in 1938 by George MacLeod, minister, visionary and prophetic witness for peace, in the context of the poverty and despair of the Depression. Its original task of rebuilding the monastic ruins of Iona Abbey became a sign of hopeful rebuilding of community in Scotland and beyond. Today, we are about 250 members, mostly in Britain, and 1500 associate members, with 1400 friends worldwide. Together and apart, 'we follow the light we have, and pray for more light'.

For information on the Iona Community contact:
The Iona Community, Fourth Floor, Savoy House, 140 Sauchiehall Street,
Glasgow G2 3DH, UK. Phone: 0141 332 6343
e-mail: admin@iona.org.uk; web: www.iona.org.uk

For enquiries about visiting Iona, please contact:
Iona Abbey, Isle of Iona, Argyll PA76 6SN, UK. Phone: 01681 700404
e-mail: ionacomm@iona.org.uk

ALSO FROM WILD GOOSE PUBLICATIONS ...

Eggs & Ashes
Practical and liturgical resources for Lent and Holy Week
Ruth Burgess & Chris Polhill

Suitable for group worship or personal reflection, and with material for Shrove Tuesday, Ash Wednesday, Mothering Sunday, Palm Sunday and Holy Week, this is a collection to accompany readers through Lent and Easter for many years. Includes a Lent discipline for those who care about the environment, liturgies, responses, prayers, poems, reflections, meditations, stories, stations of the cross, sermons, monologues and songs, with some all-age resources – written by Iona Community members, associates, friends and others.

ISBN 1 901557 87 1

Iona Dawn
Through Holy Week with the Iona Community
Neil Paynter

The dramatic events of the days leading up to Easter Sunday are expressed through biblical readings and the reflections of several well-known Iona Community members: Ruth Burgess, Jan Sutch Pickard, Tom Gordon, Brian Woodcock, Peter Millar, Kathy Galloway, Leith Fisher, Joy Mead, John Davies, Yvonne Morland. Connecting the denials, betrayals, suffering and eventual new dawn of this life-changing week with what is happening in our own world today, this book accompanies the reader as an insightful guide. To travel through Holy Week with awareness leads to a greater understanding of God and ourselves.

ISBN 1 905010 11 7

Lent & Easter Readings from Iona
Neil Paynter (ed)

This book of readings from members and staff of the Iona Community aims to help us reappraise our lives during the period leading up to Easter. Lent is traditionally a time of repentance and penitence but it also offers an opportunity to see the world afresh, with a new sense of wonder. These readings encourage us not only to regard ourselves with a healthy realism, so that we can accept responsibility for our short-comings, but also to recognise the nature and purposes of God and the never-ending renewal of possibility, both within ourselves and in the world.

ISBN 1901557626

WWW.IONABOOKS.COM

Stages on the Way
Worship Resources for Lent, Holy Week and Easter
Wild Goose Worship Group

This is the second 'book of bits' for worship produced by the Wild Goose Worship Group. It traces Jesus' road to the cross through Lent, Holy Week and Easter. Its prime purpose is to resource worship that enables people to sense the hope, apprehension and joy of Easter as felt by Jesus' friends. The range and diversity offers a unique source of elements for lay and clergy worship planners and enablers. All of the material has been used in celebrations and services of public worship, but little has been previously published.

ISBN 1901557111

Enemy of Apathy
Songbook
John L Bell/Graham Maule

Sixty-two songs and chants for Lent, Eastertide and Pentecost. Includes:
* Travelling the road to freedom
* Be still and know
* Jesus Christ is waiting
* Lord of the morning
* Kyrie/Sanctus & Benedictus/Agnus Dei (Kentigern setting)

ISBN 0947988270

A Book of Blessings
... and how to write your own
Ruth Burgess

This Wild Goose best-seller is a collection of blessings for the people, sadnesses, artefacts, special occasions and journeys of our lives. It also explores the tradition of blessings, including biblical and Celtic, and offers ideas and resources to encourage readers to write blessings of their own, with suggestions for how to organise a blessings workshop.

ISBN 1 901557 48 0

WWW.IONABOOKS.COM

Friends and Enemies
A book of short prayers & some ways to write your own
Ruth Burgess

A collection of prayers about relationships and the particular moments and places of our daily lives. They convey wisdom and humour, while some contain strong thoughts and words. 'Saying what we mean to God,' writes Ruth Burgess, 'is more honest than tiptoeing around the issues and concerns we find disturbing or difficult. To write with integrity is to write within the traditions of the writers of the psalms.' *Friends and Enemies* is offered as a resource for personal prayer and public worship, and as an encouragement to both individuals and congregations to be creative and courageous in their prayers. Includes three prayer-writing workshops.

ISBN 1 901557 78 2

Praying for the Dawn
A resource book for the ministry of healing
Ruth Burgess & Kathy Galloway

A compilation of material from several writers with strong emphasis on liturgies and resources for healing services. Includes a section on how to introduce healing services to those who may not be familiar with them, and suggestions for starting group discussions about healing. The book is rounded off by a section of worship resources – prayers, responses, litanies, poems, meditations and blessings.

ISBN 1 901557 26 X

Hay & Stardust
Resources for Christmas to Candlemas
Ruth Burgess

This companion resource book to *Candles & Conifers* covers the season of Christmastide, including Christmas Eve, Holy Innocents' Day, Winter and New Year, Epiphany, Homelessness Sunday and Candlemas. It also contains eight Christmas plays, including a puppet play.

ISBN 1 905010 00 1

WWW.IONABOOKS.COM

Candles & Conifers
Resources for All Saints' to Advent
Ruth Burgess

A collection of seasonal resources for groups and individuals – prayers, liturgies, poems, reflections, sermons, meditations, stories and responses, written by Iona Community members, associates, friends and others. It covers the weeks from All Saints' Day to Christmas Eve, including saints' days, Remembrance Day, World AIDS Day and Advent. There are liturgies for an outdoor celebration with fireworks, a Christingle service and a longest night service, as well as Advent candle ceremonies, personal prayer practices, a series of responses and blessings and a cats' Advent calendar.

ISBN 1 901557 96 0

Hear My Cry
A daily prayer book for Advent
Ruth Burgess

A daily prayer book for Advent which can also be used as a prayer journal, taking its inspiration from the Advent antiphons – a group of prayers that reflect on the character and activities of God. The format for each day includes a Bible verse, an Advent cry and suggestions for prayer. The pages can be added to and personalised, with line drawings that can be coloured in and space to add your own pictures, reflections and prayers. Instructions for three workshops are also included to enable Advent themes to be explored in a group setting.

ISBN 1 901557 95 2

Friends and Enemies
A book of short prayers & some ways to write your own
Ruth Burgess

A collection of prayers about relationships and the particular moments and places of our daily lives. They convey wisdom and humour, while some contain strong thoughts and words. 'Saying what we mean to God,' writes Ruth Burgess, 'is more honest than tiptoeing around the issues and concerns we find disturbing or difficult. To write with integrity is to write within the traditions of the writers of the psalms.' *Friends and Enemies* is offered as a resource for personal prayer and public worship, and as an encouragement to both individuals and congregations to be creative and courageous in their prayers. Includes three prayer-writing workshops.

ISBN 1 901557 78 2

WWW.IONABOOKS.COM

Wild Goose Publications, the publishing house of the Iona Community established in the Celtic Christian tradition of Saint Columba, produces books, tapes and CDs on:

- holistic spirituality
- social justice
- political and peace issues
- healing
- innovative approaches to worship
- song in worship, including the work of the Wild Goose Resource Group
- material for meditation and reflection

If you would like to find out more about our books, tapes and CDs, please contact us at:

Wild Goose Publications
Fourth Floor, Savoy House
140 Sauchiehall Street,
Glasgow G2 3DH, UK

Tel. +44 (0)141 332 6292
Fax +44 (0)141 332 1090
e-mail: admin@ionabooks.com

or visit our website at
www.ionabooks.com
for details of all our products and online sales